PRICE: $20.00 (3798/anfarp)

Also by Joan Didion

Blue Nights

The Year of Magical Thinking

We Tell Ourselves Stories in Order to Live

Where I Was From

Political Fictions

The Last Thing He Wanted

After Henry

Miami

Democracy

Salvador

The White Album

A Book of Common Prayer

Play It as It Lays

Slouching Towards Bethlehem

Run River

South and West

South and West

From a Notebook

Joan Didion

Foreword by Nathaniel Rich

Alfred A. Knopf

New York

2017

THIS IS A BORZOI BOOK
PUBLISHED BY ALFRED A. KNOPF

Copyright © 2017 by Joan Didion
Foreword copyright © 2017 by Nathaniel Rich
All rights reserved. Published in the United States by Alfred A.
Knopf, a division of Penguin Random House LLC, New York, and
distributed in Canada by Random House of Canada, a division of
Penguin Random House Limited, Toronto.

www.aaknopf.com

Knopf, Borzoi Books, and the colophon are registered trademarks of
Penguin Random House LLC.

ISBN (hardcover) 978-1-524-73279-0
ISBN (eBook) 978-1-524-73280-6

Library of Congress Control Number: 2016962161

Jacket design by Carol Devine Carson

Manufactured in the United States of America
Published February 27, 2017
Reprinted One Time
Third Printing, March 2017

Contents

ception of history. Didion's notes, which sur-
pass in elegance and clarity the finished prose
of most other writers, are a fascinating record
of this time. But they are also something more
unsettling. Readers today will recognize, with
some dismay and even horror, how much is
familiar in these long-lost American portraits.
Didion saw her era more clearly than anyone
else, which is another way of saying that she
was able to see the future.

South and West is, in one regard, the most
revealing of Didion's books. This might seem
a far-fetched claim to make about an author
who has written about her ancestry, her marriage, her health, and, with painful candor, her
grief—Didion's readers are, after all, on familiar terms with the personal details of her life.
But the writing itself—the cool majesty of her
prose, written as if from a great, even empyreal
distance, elevating personal experience into
universal revelation—has an immaculacy as
intimidating as Chelsea porcelain. *South and
West* offers for the first time a glimpse inside
the factory walls.

For each piece she reported, Didion converted pages of loose-leaf notebooks into scrapbooks of material related to her theme. She inserted newspaper articles and other writers' works, like C. Vann Woodward's "The Search for Southern Identity," biographical summaries, lists of suggested themes, and overheard dialogue, which often seems taken from one of her novels. ("I never been anyplace," says a Biloxi woman, "I wanted to go.") In her notes we learn of her "reporting tricks," which are less tricks than an intuitive genius for locating the people in a given community who will best reveal its character: the director of the local College of Cosmetology, the white owner of the black radio station, the bridal consultant of the largest department store. The notebooks also include transcriptions of her observations, which she typed at the end of each day. These notes represent an intermediate stage of writing, between shorthand and first draft, composed in an uncharacteristically casual, immediate style. There are sentences that are ideas for sentences, paragraphs that are ideas for scenes: "The land looks rich, and many people from Birmingham, etc. (rich people) maintain places here to hunt." "The country way in which he gave me names." "The resolutely 'colorful,' anecdotal quality of San Francisco history." "The sense of sports being the opiate of the people." "The sense of not being up to the landscape." The effect can be jarring, like seeing Grace Kelly photographed with her hair in rollers or hearing the demo tapes in which Brian Wilson experiments with alternative arrangements of "Good Vibrations."

Yet even in its most casual iteration, Didion's voice, with its sensitivity to the grotesqueries and vanities that dance beneath the skim of daily experience, is unmistakable. The New Orleans atmosphere "never reflects light but sucks it in until random objects glow with a morbid luminescence." The audience dutifully watching *Loving* at the movie theater in Meridian gazes at the screen "as if the movie were Czech." The rivers are always brown and still: "A sense," she writes, "of water moccasins." Didion's implacable fatalism is at home in the South, particularly in New Orleans:

"Bananas would rot, and harbor tarantulas. Weather would come in on the radar, and be bad. Children would take fever and die."

She made her tour in a rental car but the road-trip aspect is barely commented upon; instead we have the surreal image of Didion swimming her way across the Gulf South through its motel pools. At the Edgewater Gulf Hotel pool in Biloxi "the water smells of fish," at the Howard Johnson's in Meridian a child dries off in a Confederate-flag beach towel, at the Ramada Inn in Tuscaloosa "everything seemed to be made of concrete, and damp," in Winfield the pool is filled with algae, at the Oxford Holiday Inn the broadcast of a radio station can be heard underwater, and at the St. Francis Motel in Birmingham, her bikini attracts excited comment from the bar. Lying poolside, she feels "the euphoria of Interstate America: I could be in San Bernardino, or Phoenix, or outside Indianapolis," but these motels have the appearance of stage sets. They are American markers artificially planted in the brooding wildness of the Deep South, which in these notes resembles a foreign country as exotic as El Salvador, Vietnam, Granada, or the other tropics "of morbidity and paranoia and fantasy" to which she gravitated in her nonfiction and fiction.

Even the glimpses of unlikely beauty—the wild carrots growing around the raised railroad tracks in Biloxi, the small girl sitting in the sawdust stringing pop tops from beer cans into a necklace—contribute to the general atmosphere of uneasiness, rot, and "somnolence so dense it seemed to inhibit breathing." There is a long tradition of northern visitors seeing in the Gulf South an atmosphere of perpetual decline, in which "everything seems to go to seed." Didion quotes Audubon's line about "the dangerous nature of the ground, its oozing, spongy and miry disposition," though you could go back to 1720, when a visiting French official described the territory as "flooded, unhealthy, impracticable." Didion is on narrower footing, however, when she describes her central thesis:

a sense which struck me now and then, and which I could not explain coherently, that

for some years the South and particularly
the Gulf Coast had been for America what
people were still saying California was, and
what California seemed to me not to be: the
future, the secret source of malevolent and
benevolent energy, the psychic center.

How could the hidebound South, with its
perpetual disintegration and defiant deca-
dence, at the same time represent the future?
Didion admits the idea seems oxymoronic,
but she is onto something. Part of the answer,
she suspects, lies in the bluntness with
which Southerners confront race, class, and
heritage—"distinctions which the frontier
ethic teaches western children to deny, and
to leave deliberately unmentioned." In the
South such distinctions are visible, rigid, and
the subject of frank conversation. She visits
Stan Torgerson, the owner of Meridian's "ethnic station," who programs gospel and soul
and a show called *Adventures in Black History,*
"to point out the contributions black people
have made." He speaks of the importance of
increased minimum wage and education fund-

ing, while being careful not to overstate his own open-mindedness. "I'm not saying I'm going to have a black minister come home to dinner tonight," he tells her, as they drive through the deserted downtown, "'cause I'm not." Didion encounters the same conception of social order at the Mississippi Broadcasters' awards banquet, where the lieutenant governor decries violent campus protests, and in Birmingham where someone jokes about the "feudal situation" in which white tenants live on wealthy country estates. Everybody in the South knows where they stand. There is no shame in discussing it. It is suspicious, in fact, to avoid the subject.

This kind of thinking seemed retrograde in the seventies. From the vantage of New York, California, even New Orleans, it still seems so today. But this southern frame of mind has annexed territory in the last four decades, expanding across the Mason-Dixon Line into the rest of rural America. It has taken root among people—or at least registered voters— nostalgic for a more orderly past in which the men concentrated on hunting and fishing and the women on "their cooking, their canning, their 'prettifying' "; when graft as a way of life was accepted, particularly in politics, and segregation was unquestioned; when a white supremacist running for public office was "a totally explicable phenomenon"; when a wife knew better than to travel through strange territory with a bikini and without a wedding ring.

An unquestioned premise among those who live in American cities with international airports has been, for more than half a century now, that Enlightenment values would in time become conventional wisdom. Some fought for this future to come sooner. Others waited patiently. But nobody seemed to believe that it would never arrive. Nobody, certainly, in Los Angeles or the Bay Area, which since Didion's reporting has only accelerated in its embrace of an ethic in which the past is fluid, meaningless, neutered by technological advancement. In this view the past is relegated to the aesthetic realm, to what Didion describes in "California Notes" as "decorative touches"— tastefully aged cutlery and window curtains.

In this view the past was safely dead and could not return to bloody the land.

Two decades into the new millennium, however, a plurality of the population has clung defiantly to the old way of life. They still believe in the viability of armed revolt. As Didion herself noted nearly fifty years ago, their solidarity is only reinforced by outside disapproval, particularly disapproval by the northern press. They have resisted with mockery, then rage, the collapse of the old identity categories. They have resisted the premise that white skin should not be given special consideration. They have resisted new technology and scientific evidence of global ecological collapse. The force of this resistance has been strong enough to elect a president.

A writer from the Gulf South once wrote that the past is not even past. Didion goes further, suggesting that the past was also the future. Now that we live in that future, her observations read like a warning unheeded. They suggest that California's dreamers of the golden dream were just that—dreamers—while the "dense obsessiveness" of the South, and all

the vindictiveness that comes with it, was
the true American condition, the condition
to which we will always inevitably return.
Joan Didion went to the South to understand
something about California and she ended up
understanding something about America.

—Nathaniel Rich
New Orleans
December 2016

Notes on the South

John and I were living on Franklin Avenue in Los Angeles. I had wanted to revisit the South, so we flew there for a month in 1970. The idea was to start in New Orleans and from there we had no plan. We went wherever the day took us. I seem to remember that John drove. I had not been back since 1942–43, when my father was stationed in Durham, North Carolina, but it did not seem to have changed that much. At the time, I had thought it might be a piece.

New Orleans

In New Orleans in June the air is heavy with sex and death, not violent death but death by decay, overripeness, rotting, death by drowning, suffocation, fever of unknown etiology. The place is physically dark, dark like the negative of a photograph, dark like an X-ray: the atmosphere absorbs its own light, never reflects light but sucks it in until random objects glow with a morbid luminescence. The crypts above ground dominate certain vistas. In the hypnotic liquidity of the atmosphere all motion slows into choreography, all people on the street move as if suspended in a precarious emulsion, and there seems only a technical distinction between the quick and the dead.

One afternoon on St. Charles Avenue I saw a woman die, fall forward over the wheel of her car. "Dead," pronounced an old woman who stood with me on the sidewalk a few inches from where the car had veered into a tree. After the police ambulance came I followed the old woman through the aqueous light of the Pontchartrain Hotel garage and into the coffee shop. The death had seemed serious but casual, as if it had taken place in a pre-Columbian city where death was expected, and did not in the long run count for much.

"Whose fault is it," the old woman was saying to the waitress in the coffee shop, her voice trailing off.

"It's nobody's fault, Miss Clarice."

"They can't help it, no."

"They can't help at all." I had thought they were talking about the death but they were talking about the weather. "Richard used to work at the Bureau and he told me, they can't help what comes in on the radar." The waitress paused, as if for emphasis. "They simply cannot be held to account."

"They just can't," the old woman said.

"It comes in on the radar."

The words hung in the air. I swallowed a piece of ice.

"And we get it," the old woman said after a while.

It was a fatalism I would come to recognize as endemic to the particular tone of New Orleans life. Bananas would rot, and harbor tarantulas. Weather would come in on the radar, and be bad. Children would take fever and die, domestic arguments would end in knifings, the construction of highways would lead to graft and cracked pavement where the vines would shoot back. Affairs of state would turn on sexual jealousy, in New Orleans as if in Port-au-Prince, and all the king's men would turn on the king. The temporality of the place is operatic, childlike, the fatalism that of a culture dominated by wilderness. "All we know," said the mother of Carl Austin Weiss of the son who had just shot and killed Huey Long in a corridor of the Louisiana State Capitol Building in Baton Rouge, "is that he took living seriously."

As it happens I was taught to cook by someone from Louisiana, where an avid preoccupation with recipes and food among men was not unfamiliar to me. We lived together for some years, and I think we most fully understood each other when once I tried to kill him with a kitchen knife. I remember spending whole days cooking with N., perhaps the most pleasant days we spent together. He taught me to fry chicken and to make a brown rice stuffing for fowl and to chop endive with garlic and lemon juice and to lace everything I did with Tabasco and Worcestershire and black pepper. The first present he ever gave me was a garlic press, and also the second, because I broke the first. One day on the Eastern Shore we spent hours making shrimp bisque and then had an argument about how much salt it needed, and because he had been drinking Sazeracs for several hours he poured salt in to make his point. It was like brine, but we pretended it was fine. Throwing the chicken on the floor, or the artichoke. Buying crab boil. Discussing endlessly the possibilities of an artichoke-and-oyster casserole. After I married he still called me up occasionally for recipes.

I guess you think this is a better machine than that Wop affair. I guess you think you have redwood flagstones in your backyard. I guess you think your mother used to be County Cookie Chairman. I guess you think I take up a lot of room in a small bed. I guess you think Schrafft's has chocolate leaves. I guess you think Mr. Earl "Elbow" Reum has more personality than I. I guess you think there are no lesbians in Nevada. I guess you think you know how to wash

sweaters by hand. I guess you think you
get picked on by Mary Jane and that
people serve you bad whiskey. I guess
you think you haven't got pernicious
anemia. Take those vitamins. I guess
you think southerners are somewhat
anachronistic.

—is a message that man left me when I was
twenty-two.

The first time I was ever in the South was in
late 1942, early 1943. My father was stationed
in Durham, North Carolina, and my mother
and brother and I took a series of slow and
overcrowded trains to meet him there. At home
in California I had cried at night, I had lost
weight, I had wanted my father. I had imagined
the Second World War as a punishment specifically designed to deprive me of my father, had
counted up my errors and, with an egocentric-
ity which then approached autism and which
afflicts me still in dreams and fevers and marriage, found myself guilty.

Of the trip I recall mainly that a sailor who
had just been torpedoed on the *Wasp* in the

Pacific gave me a silver-and-turquoise ring, and that we missed our connection in New Orleans and could get no room and sat up one night on a covered verandah of the St. Charles Hotel, my brother and I in matching seersucker sunsuits and my mother in a navy-blue-and-white-checked silk dress dusty from the train. She covered us with the mink coat she had bought before her marriage and wore until 1956. We were taking trains instead of driving because a few weeks before in California she had lent the car to an acquaintance who drove it into a lettuce truck outside Salinas, a fact of which I am certain because it remains a source of rancor, in my father's dialogue, to this day. I last heard it mentioned a week ago. My mother made no response, only laid out another hand of solitaire.

In Durham we had one room with kitchen privileges in the house of a lay minister whose children ate apple butter on thick slabs of bread all day long and referred to their father in front of us as "Reverend Caudill." In the evenings Reverend Caudill would bring home five or six quarts of peach ice cream, and he and his wife and children would sit on the front porch spooning peach ice cream from the cartons while we lay in our room watching our mother read and waiting for Thursday.

Thursday was the day we could take the bus to Duke University, which had been taken over by the military, and spend the afternoon with my father. He would buy us a Coca-Cola in the student union and walk us around the campus and take snapshots of us, which I now have, and look at from time to time: two small children and a woman who resembles me, sitting by the lagoon, standing by the wishing well, the snapshots always lightstruck or badly focused and, in any case, now faded. Thirty years later I am certain that my father must also have been with us on weekends, but I can only suggest that his presence in the small house, his tension and his aggressive privacy and his preference for shooting craps over eating peach ice cream, must have seemed to me so potentially disruptive as to efface all memory of weekends.

On the days of the week which were not Thursday I played with a set of paper dolls lent me by Mrs. Caudill, the dolls bearing the faces of Vivien Leigh, Olivia de Havilland, Ann Rutherford, and Butterfly McQueen as they appeared in *Gone With the Wind,* and I also learned from the neighborhood children to eat raw potatoes dipped in the soft dust from beneath the house. I know now that eating pica is common in the undernourished South, just as I know now why the driver of the bus on the first Thursday we went out to Duke refused to leave the curb until we had moved from the back seat to the front, but I did not know it then. I did not even know then that my mother found our sojourn of some months in Durham less than ideal.

I could never precisely name what impelled me to spend time in the South during the summer of 1970. There was no reportorial imperative to any of the places I went at the time I went: nothing "happened" anywhere I was, no celebrated murders, trials, integration orders, confrontations, not even any celebrated acts of God.

I had only some dim and unformed sense,
a sense which struck me now and then, and
which I could not explain coherently, that for
some years the South and particularly the Gulf
Coast had been for America what people were
still saying California was, and what California
seemed to me not to be: the future, the secret
source of malevolent and benevolent energy,
the psychic center. I did not much want to talk
about this.

I had only the most ephemeral "picture" in
my mind. If I talked about it I could mention
only Clay Shaw, and Garrison, and a pilot I
had once met who flew between the Gulf and
unnamed Caribbean and Central American
airstrips for several years on small planes with
manifests that showed only "tropical flowers,"
could mention only some apprehension of
paranoia and febrile conspiracy and baroque
manipulation and peach ice cream and an
unpleasant evening I had spent in 1962 on the
Eastern Shore of Maryland. In short I could
only sound deranged. And so instead of talking about it I flew south one day in the summer
of 1970, rented a car, and drove for a month or

so around Louisiana and Mississippi and Alabama, saw no spokesmen, covered no events, did nothing at all but try to find out, as usual, what was making the picture in my mind.

In New Orleans, the old people sitting in front of houses and hotels on St. Charles Avenue, barely rocking. In the Quarter I saw them again (along with desolate long-haired children), sitting on balconies, an ironing board behind them, gently rocking, sometimes not rocking at all but only staring. In New Orleans they have mastered the art of the motionless.

In the evening I visited in the Garden District. "Olly olly oxen free" echoing in the soft twilight, around the magnolias and the trees with fluffy pods of pink. What I saw that night was a world so rich and complex and I was almost disoriented, a world complete unto itself, a world of smooth surfaces broken occasionally by a flash of eccentricity so deep that it numbed any attempt at interpretation.

"I guess nobody knows more about the South

than the people in this room right now," my host allowed several times before dinner. We were at his house in the Garden District with the requisite bound volumes of the *Sewanee* and the *Southern Review* and the requisite Degas portrait of his great-great-grandmother, and he was talking about his wife and their friend, an architect of good Mobile family who specialized in the restoration and building of New Orleans Greek Revival houses.

And of course he was talking about himself. "Ben C.," the others called him, their voices fondly inflected. "You just *stop* that, Ben C.," as he bullied the two women, his sister and his wife working together on a Junior League project, a guidebook to New Orleans. Already Ben C. had demanded to know what "athletics" my husband played, and why I had been allowed, in the course of doing some reporting a few years before, to "spend time consorting with a lot of marijuana-smoking hippie trash."

"Who allowed you?" he repeated.

I said that I did not know quite what he meant.

Ben C. only stared at me.

"I mean, who wouldn't have allowed me?"

"You *do* have a husband?" he said finally. "This man I've thought was your husband for several years, he *is* your husband?"

The evening, it developed, had started off wrong for Ben C. It seemed that he had called some of his cousins to come for dinner, and they had made excuses, and he had found that "inexcusable." It further seemed that the excuse made by one cousin, who it would turn out was a well-known southern writer, was a previous engagement with the director of a Head Start program, and Ben C. had found that particularly inexcusable.

"What am I meant to conclude?" he demanded rhetorically of his wife. "Am I meant to conclude he's certifiable?"

"Maybe you're meant to conclude he didn't care to come to dinner," she said, and then, as if to cover her irreverence, she sighed. "I only hope he doesn't get too mixed up with the Negroes. You know what happened to George Washington Cable."

I tried to remember what had happened to George Washington Cable.

"He ended up having to go *north,* is what happened."

I said that I wanted only to know what people in the South were thinking and doing.

He continued to gaze at me. He had the smooth, rounded face of well-off New Orleans, that absence of angularity which characterizes the local genetic pool. I tried to think who had incurred his wrath by going up north and whining.

"I would just guess that we know a little more about the subject," Ben C. said finally, his voice rising, "than one Mr. Willie Morris."

We ate trout with shallots and mushrooms. We drank some white wine, we drank some more bourbon. We passed the evening. I never learned why the spectre of one Mr. Willie Morris had materialized in that living room in the Garden District, nor did I ask.

Ben C.'s wife and sister, Mrs. Benjamin C. Toledano and Mrs. Beauregard Redmond, soon to be Mrs. Toledano Redmond, had many suggestions for understanding the South. I must walk Bourbon or Royal to Chartres, I must walk Chartres to Esplanade. I must have coffee and doughnuts at the French Market. I should not miss St. Louis Cathedral, the Presbytère, the Cabildo. We should have lunch at Galatoire's: trout amandine or trout Marguery. We should obtain a copy of *The Great Days of the Garden District.* We should visit Asphodel, Rosedown, Oakley Plantation. Stanton Hall in Natchez. The Grand Hotel in Point Clear. We should have dinner at Manale's, tour Coliseum Square Park. I should appreciate the grace, the beauty of their way of life. These graceful preoccupations seemed to be regarded by the women in a spirit at once dedicated and merely tolerant, as if they lived their lives on several quite contradictory levels.

One afternoon we took the ferry to Algiers and drove an hour or so down the river, in Plaquemines Parish. This is peculiar country. Algiers is a doubtful emulsion of white frame bungalows and jerry-built apartment complexes, the Parc Fontaine Apts. and so forth, and the drive on down the river takes you through a landscape more metaphorical than any I have seen outside the Sonoran Desert.

Here and there one is conscious of the levee, off to the left. Corn and tomatoes grow aimlessly, as if naturalized. I am too accustomed to agriculture as agribusiness, the rich vistas of the California valleys where all the resources of Standard Oil and the University of California have been brought to bear on glossy constant productivity. No Hunting of Quadrupeds, a sign read in Belle Chasse. What could that mean? Can you hunt reptiles? Bipeds? There are dead dogs by the road, and a sinking graveyard in a grove of live oak.

Getting close to Port Sulphur we began to see sulphur works, the tanks glowing oddly in the peculiar light. We ran over three snakes in the hour's drive, one of them a thick black moccasin already dead, twisted across the one lane. There were run-down antiques places, and tomato stands, and a beauty shop called Feminine Fluff. The snakes, the rotting undergrowth, sulphurous light: the images are so specifically those of the nightmare world that when we stopped for gas, or directions, I had to steel myself, deaden every nerve, in order to step from the car onto the crushed oyster shells in front of the gas station. When we got back to the hotel I stood in the shower for almost half an hour trying to wash myself clean of the afternoon, but then I started thinking about where the water came from, what dark places it had pooled in.

When I think now about New Orleans I remember mainly its dense obsessiveness, its vertiginous preoccupation with race, class, heritage, style, and the absence of style. As it happens, these particular preoccupations all involve distinctions which the frontier ethic teaches western children to deny and to leave deliberately unmentioned, but in New Orleans such distinctions are the basis of much conversation, and lend that conversation its peculiar childlike cruelty and innocence. In New Orleans they also talk about parties, and about food, their voices rising and falling, never still, as if talking about anything at all could keep the wilderness at bay. In New Orleans the wilderness is sensed as very near, not the redemptive wilderness of the western imagina-

tion but something rank and old and malevolent, the idea of wilderness not as an escape
from civilization and its discontents but as
a mortal threat to a community precarious
and colonial in its deepest aspect. The effect
is lively and avaricious and intensely self-
absorbed, a tone not uncommon in colonial
cities, and the principal reason I find such cities invigorating.

New Orleans to Biloxi, Mississippi

On the Chef Menteur Highway out of New
Orleans there is the sense of swamp reclaimed
to no point. Dismal subdivisions evoke the
romance of Evangeline on their billboards.
Shacks along the road sell plaster statues of
the Virgin Mary. The gas stations advertise
Free Flag Decals. Lake Pontchartrain can be
seen now and then on the left, and the rusted
hulks of boats at marine repair places.

The rest of it is swamp. Crude signs point down dirt roads, and along the road are shacks, or "camps," for fishing. Postboxes are supported on twisted rigid chains, as if the inhabitants are as conscious as the traveler of the presence of snakes. The light is odd, more peculiar still than the light in New Orleans, light entirely absorbed by what it strikes.

We stopped at a trinket shack called the Beachcomber. A boy was filling the Pepsi machine outside. Towels hung limply on a display clothesline: "Put Your (picture of a HEART) in Dixie or Get Your (picture of an ASS) OUT!" Inside were boxes of shells and dried devilfish. "They get 'em from Mexico," the boy said.

Across the Mississippi line we took a side road through the pine forest toward what the sign said would be E. Ansley Estates. Rain was beginning to fall, and as we passed a pond a dozen or so boys were climbing out of the water and into two cars. One felt the rain had spoiled their day, and they would be at loose ends, restless. The cliché of the lonely road in the South took on a certain meaning here. The road was scattered occasionally with armadillo shells. The rain continued. The boys and their cars disappeared. We did not find E. Ansley Estates, or any settlement at all.

Signs for fireworks, signs for a reptile farm ahead. The rain let up and we stopped at the reptile farm. The Reptile House was a small shack out in back of the main roadside building, across a dirt yard where chickens ran loose. The place was dirty, littered with peanut shells and empty six-pack cartons marked Dad's Root Beer and Suncrest Orange Drink. There were a few capuchin monkeys, and a couple of big lethargic boas in packing cases, and a Holbrook's king snake and a couple of rattlers. A cage marked COPPERHEAD appeared to be empty. There was a family in the Reptile House when we were there, a boy about nine and a father and a woman in slacks with her hair piled high and lacquered.

We stood, the five of us, and looked restlessly out into the driving rain, trapped together in the Reptile House. The dust outside was turning to deep mud. Alligators thrashed in a muddy pool a few yards away. A little farther a sign said Snake Pit.

"I never would've stopped if I'd known it was outside," the woman said.

"Known what was outside?" her husband said.

"The Snake Pit, of course. What do you *think* is outside?"

The man drummed his fingers on top of a packing case. The boa inside slid deeper into its coil. To make conversation I asked the man if they had visited a far building marked Reptile House.

"There aren't no reptiles upstairs there," he said, and then, as if I might doubt it: "She told us, there aren't no reptiles upstairs. She said not to go in."

"Maybe there are some reptiles downstairs?" I suggested.

"I don't know about that," he said. "I just wouldn't go in."

"Of course *you* wouldn't," the woman said mildly. She was still staring at the Snake Pit.

I was leaning on the empty copperhead box listening to the rain hiss when an uneasy feeling came over me that the hissing came from inside the box. I looked again and there it was, a copperhead, almost hidden by its shed skins.

We gave up on one another, and on the possibility of the rain's stopping, and ran through the mud back to the main house. I slipped and fell in the mud and had an instant of irrational panic that there were snakes in the mud and all around me.

In the trinket shop the woman and I each paid a dime to use the restroom. With another dime I got a cup of cold coffee from a machine and tried to stop being chilled. The woman bought her son a china potty with a little child disappearing down the drain and the inscription "Goodbye Sweet World." I bought a cheap beach towel printed with a Confederate flag. It is ragged and gray now and sits in my linen closet in California amid thick and delicately colored Fieldcrest beach towels, and my child prefers it to the good ones.

Pass Christian to Gulfport

At Pass Christian in the summer of 1970 the debris of the 1969 hurricane had become the natural look of the landscape. The big houses along the water were abandoned, the schools and churches were wiped out, the windows of places hung askew. The devastation along the Gulf had an inevitability about it: the coast was reverting to its natural state. There were For Sale signs all over, but one could not imagine buyers. I remembered people talking about Pass Christian as a summer place, and indeed the houses had once been pretty and white and the American flags unfaded, but even in the good years there must have been an uneasiness there. They sat on those screened porches and waited for something to happen. The place must have always failed at being a resort, if the special quality of a resort is defined as security: there is here that ominous white/dark light so characteristic of the entire Gulf.

The city hall in Pass Christian faces away from the Gulf, and when you happen upon it from the front it looks like a façade from a studio back lot, abandoned a long time ago. Through the shattered windows one sees the dark glare of the Gulf. You want to close your eyes.

Long Beach seemed poorer, or harder hit, or both. There were none of those big white houses with the screened porches here. There were trailers, and a twisted pool ladder that marked the place where a swimming pool had been before the hurricane. Mass was being held in the school gym. On the beach there was an occasional woman with children. The women wore two-piece bathing suits, shorts and halters, not bikinis. All along the coast there were cars parked and tables set up to sell colored discs that whir in the air, apparently indefinitely. On the cars are hand-lettered signs that read SPACE STATION. You can see discs shimmering in the light from a long way off.

At Gulfport, the county seat of Harrison

County, a tanker, broken clean in half during the hurricane, lay rusting offshore. The heat was relentless, the streets downtown broad and devoid of trees. *The Losers* was playing at the Sand Theatre in Gulfport, and would be playing at The Avenue in Biloxi. We went into a café downtown to get something to eat. CAFÉ is all the sign said. The menu had red beans and rice, and the only sounds in the place in the afternoon stillness were the whirring of the air conditioner and the click of a pinball machine. Everyone in the place seemed to have been there a long time, and to know everyone else. After a while a man got up from his beer and walked to the door. "Off to the infirmary," he said over his shoulder.

Between Gulfport and Biloxi, the shingles were ripped from the houses facing the Gulf. Live oak trees were twisted and broken. A long way in the distance one could see the Biloxi Lighthouse, a white tower glowing peculiarly in the strange afternoon light.

I had never expected to come to the Gulf Coast married.

Biloxi

Everything seems to go to seed along the Gulf: walls stain, windows rust. Curtains mildew. Wood warps. Air conditioners cease to function. In our room at the Edgewater Gulf Hotel, where the Mississippi Broadcasters' Convention was taking place, the air conditioner in the window violently shook and rattled every time it was turned on. The Edgewater Gulf is an enormous white hotel which looks like a giant laundry, and has the appearance of being on the verge of condemnation. The swimming pool is large and unkempt, and the water smells of fish. Behind the hotel is a new shopping center built around an air-conditioned mall, and I kept escaping there, back into midstream America.

In the elevator at the Edgewater Gulf:

"Walter, I believe you've grown the most of any town in the state of Mississippi."

"Well, the figures are in question."

"Didn't quite total as high as the chamber of commerce thought they would?"

"No, well—"

"Same in Tupelo. In Tupelo they demanded a recount."

"Well, frankly, I don't think we've got all those people . . . they see the cars, they think they live here, but they come in from around, spend a dollar a day—"

"Dollar, top."

The two men faced the front of the elevator as they spoke, not each other. The dialogue was grave. The possibility of "growth" in small Mississippi towns is ever yearned for, and ever denied. The Mississippi Broadcasters' was, everyone assured me, "the best damn convention in the state of Mississippi."

One evening after dinner we drove around Biloxi, and stopped to watch a Pony League game being played under bright lights. A handful of men in short-sleeved shirts and women in faded cotton blouses and Capri pants sat in the bleachers, watching the children play, Holiday Inn versus Burger Chef. Below the bleachers some children played barefoot in the dust, and a police car was parked, its motor idling, its doors open. There was no one in the car. The game broke up finally, to no one's satisfaction.

There are railroad tracks running through all the towns in Mississippi, or so it seems, and at every crossing is a sign that reads MISSIS-SIPPI LAW/STOP. The tracks are raised and the wild carrot grows around them.

After the Pony League game broke up we went to get a beer in a bar a few blocks away, and there were some of the other people from the bleachers, and no children in evidence. It was apparently just a way to pass a few hours on a summer evening. They had already seen *The Losers*, say, and it was hot in the house, and supper was finished at sundown.

Another way to pass the time that evening (but I believe it was an almost imperceptibly more middle-class pastime) was at the Kiwanis Fishing Rodeo, where the biggest fish caught that day were displayed in trays of ice. In the sawdust under the awning a small girl sat, stringing the pop tops from beer cans into a necklace.

One morning at 10:30 a.m. during the Mississippi Broadcasters' Convention there was, in the ballroom of the Edgewater Gulf, an event designated on the program as the Ladies' Brunch. The Billy Fane Trio played, and Bob McRaney, Sr., of WROB West Point, presided. "The Billy Fane Trio is becoming something of an institution as regards our convention," he said, and then he introduced another act: "We have an act this morning that ... I think ... unless you've been an Indian on a reservation and not many of us have ... you'll find rather novel and unusual to say the least. Out in Colorado ... or out somewhere in the West there ... there's a very quaint little village named Taos. And we have a young man this morning who has perfected a Taos Hoop Dance ... It's Allen Thomas, from Franklinton, Louisiana, ... with Martin Belcher on the Indian drums."

"You'll love this act," someone at my table said. "We saw it at the high school up on 49."

"I wish I could play organ like that," someone else said when the Billy Fane Trio was playing.

"Don't you, though?"

"You-all ought to come visit with us," a third woman said. They were all young women, the oldest among them perhaps thirty. "I'd play organ for you."

"We'll never get up there," the first woman said. "I never been anyplace I wanted to go."

A drawing was held for door prizes, the first prize being a room paneled in Masonite. The women genuinely wanted the Masonite room, and they also wanted the carving set, the playing cards, the pair of Miss America shoes, the lighted cosmetic mirror, and the woodcut of Christ. They recalled among them who had won door prizes in years past, and their wistful envy of each winner suffused the room. Little girls in sandals and sundresses played at the edge of the ballroom, waiting for their mothers, who were now, during the drawing, as children themselves.

The isolation of these people from the currents of American life in 1970 was startling and bewildering to behold. All their information was fifth-hand, and mythicized in the handing down. Does it matter where Taos is, after all, if Taos is not in Mississippi?

At the Mississippi Broadcasters' awards banquet, there were many jokes and parables. Here is a joke: "Can you tell me what you'd get if you crossed a violin with a rooster? The answer is, if you looked out in your chicken yard you might see someone fiddling around with your rooster." This seemed to me an interesting joke, in that no element of it was amusing, yet everyone roared, and at tables all around me it was repeated for those who had missed the punch line.

And here is a parable I heard that night: "There was a bee buzzing in a clover field, and a cow came along and swallowed the bee, and the bee buzzed around and it was warm and sleepy and the bee went to sleep, and when the bee woke up, the cow was gone." As I recall, this parable illustrated some point about broadcasting good tidings rather than bad, and it seemed to make the point very clearly to the audience, but it continued to elude me.

Someone at the rostrum mentioned repeatedly that we were "entering the space age in the new decade," but we seemed very far from that, and in any case had we not already entered the space age? I had the feeling that I had been too long on the Gulf Coast, that my own sources of information were distant and removed, that like the women at the Ladies' Brunch I might never get anywhere I wanted to go. One of the awards that night was for the Best Program Series by a Female.

The luncheon was honoring Congressman William Colmer (D-Miss.), who had been thirty-eight years in the House and was chairman of the House Rules Committee. He was receiving the Broadcasters' Man of the Year award, and had come with his AA, his mother, and his secretary. In accepting his award Rep. Colmer murmured something about "bad apples in every lot," and, about the interest of the rest of the nation in the state of Mississippi, "like havin' an obstetrician in New Jersey when the baby's bein' born in Mississippi."

"We get a lot of bad publicity down here," said someone accepting a Distinguished Public Service award. The solidarity engendered by outside disapproval, a note struck constantly. It seemed to have reached a point where all

Mississippians were bonded together in a way simply not true of the residents of any other state. They could be comfortable only with each other. Any differences they might have, class or economic or even in a real way racial, seemed outweighed by what they shared.

Charles L. Sullivan, introduced as "lieutenant governor of the state of Mississippi and a member of the Clarksdale Baptist Church," rose to speak. "I have come to think we are living in the era of the demonstrators—unruly, unwashed, uninformed, and sometimes un-American people—disrupting private and public life in this country." He complained of the press, "for whom two loud 'Ah Hate Mississippis' would be sufficient. This adult generation accomplished more than any generation in the history of civilization—it started the exploration of God's limitless space. I simply will not hear them cry Pig for a situation they themselves began. Ah don't believe the right to disagree is the right to destroy the University at Jackson or Kent State or [the "even" was implicit] Berkeley. If it is true, as they say, that they have despaired of the democratic process, then I and my fellow demonstrators shall absolutely insist that if our system is to be changed it shall be changed in the ballot box and not in the streets." He finally ended on the rote ending to southern speeches: "We can live together in the dignity and freedom which their Creator surely intended."

With many of the Highway Patrol as honored guests there was an undertone to this lunch and throughout his speech, since it was the Highway Patrol who had done the shooting at Jackson.

Random notes from the weekend: The black station manager from Gulfport standing in line talking to Stan Torgerson from Meridian about black programming, Torgerson saying he programs Top 40, no deep blues or soul, and he owns a record store too "so I know goddamn well what they buy." Bob Evans from WNAG Grenada, trying to explain the class structure of Mississippi towns in terms of five families, with the banker always number one because he makes the loans. A black girl, a student at Jackson State, presented a list of demands at an afternoon meeting and everyone explained to me that she did it "very courteously." A tribute to coverage during Hurricane Camille, "Broadcasting working in symphonic harmony with the weather bureau and the civil defense authorities." After that crisis "celebrities from all over the U.S. came down, Bob Hope, the Golddiggers, Bobby Goldsboro. Bob Hope coming down, that really made people see that the country cared." Mrs. McGrath from Jackson leaning close to tell me Jackson State was a setup.

The Gulf Coast resorts live to a certain extent on illegal gambling, places back up in the pinewoods known to all visitors. The Mafia is strong on the Coast.

The Ladies at the Brunch, on the subject of TV:

"I keep it on for my stories."

"Need to have it for the stories."

"I hear the radio only in the kitchen."

How about driving, I asked. The pretty young woman looked at me as if truly bewildered.

"Drive where?" she asked.

I did not know why we were going to Meridian instead of Mobile as planned, but it seemed, after a few days, imperative to leave the Gulf and the steaming air.

On the Road from Biloxi to Meridian

There was occasional rain and an overcast sky and the raw piney woods. On an AM station out of Biloxi, 1400 on the dial, I listened to Richard Brannan tell a parable about "a sailing trip to the Bahama Islands." The radio was out, but finally they got a fix and headed for port. "Everybody gets happy when the right direction is found," he said. "I mention this because there is another ship in danger of losing its way . . . the old ship of state." Then they played "America the Beautiful" with an angel choir. It was a Sunday. Here and all over were the trailer-sales lots with the signs that said REPOSSESSIONS, the trailers bearing plates from all over the South.

In McHenry, Mississippi, a gas station and a few shacks and a dirt road leading back into the pines, three barefoot children played in the

dust by the gas station. A little girl with long
unkempt blond hair and a dirty periwinkle-
blue dress that hung below her knees carried
around an empty Sprite bottle. The older of
the two boys got the Coke machine open and
they all squabbled gently over their choices.
A pickup pulled in with the back piled high
with broken furniture and dirty mattresses: it
sometimes seemed to me that mattresses were
on the move all over the South. A middle-aged
blond woman was pumping gas. "One of the
boys is off today, so they got me working," she
said. We drove on, past cattle, a Church of
God, a Jax (Fabacher) beer sign, and the Wig-
gin Lumber Co. Mfrs. Southern Yellow Pine
Lumber.

A somnolence so dense it seemed to inhibit
breathing hung over Hattiesburg, Mississippi,
at two or three o'clock of that Sunday afternoon. There was no place to get lunch, no place
to get gas. On the wide leafy streets the white
houses were set back. Sometimes I would see
a face at a window. I saw no one on the streets.

Outside Hattiesburg we stopped at a CAFÉ–
GAS–TRUCK STOP to get a sandwich. A blond

girl with a pellagra face stood sullenly behind the cash register, and a couple of men sat in a booth. Behind the counter was a woman in a pink Dacron housedress. No flicker of expression crossed her classic mountain face, and her movements were so slow as to be hypnotic. She made a kind of ballet of scooping ice into a glass. Behind her a soft-ice-cream machine oozed and plopped, and every now and then ice cubes would fall in the ice machine. Neither she nor the girl nor the two men spoke during the time we were there. The jukebox played "Sweet Caroline." They all watched me eat a grilled-cheese sandwich. When we went back out into the blazing heat one of the men followed us and watched as we drove away.

In Laurel, pop. 29,000: FREE FLAG DE-CALS, as everywhere. PUMP YOUR OWN GAS SAVE 5¢. It's Fun. Shacks on the backstreets. A black woman sitting on her front porch on the backseat from a car.

Cannibalized rusting automobiles everywhere, in ditches, the kudzu taking over. White wild flowers, red dirt. The pines here are getting lower, bushier. Polled Herefords.

NOTES ON THE SOUTH

In a time when we have come to associate untouched land with parkland, a luxury, Mississippi seemed rich in appearance. One forgets that this is pre-industrial, not parkland purchased at great cost in an industrial society. There is very little of this hill land under the least cultivation. A patch of corn here, but nothing else.

A few signs in Enterprise, Mississippi: SEVEN HAMBURGERS FOR $1. FOOTLONG BARBECUE 30¢. People sitting on the porches.

Basic City, Mississippi, a town not on the map. You go in on a road and there, at the confluence of two railroad tracks, is a quite beautiful white frame house with a green lawn and gazebo. Lacy white flowers. The eccentricity of its location renders the viewer speechless. Across one set of tracks is a sign: PRIVATE DOGWOOD SPRINGS M.E. SKELTON'S FAMILY, OWNER. BASIC CITY MISS. Back on the road, the road into Meridian, 11, is the BASIC COURT CAFÉ AIR COND. When I left Basic City a train was moaning, the Meridian & Bigbee line. One is conscious of trains in the South. It is a true earlier time.

Swimming at the Howard Johnson's in Meridian

The Howard Johnson's in Meridian is just off Interstate 20, the intersection of Interstate 20—running east and west—and Interstate 59—running north and south from New Orleans to New York. Population 58,000, and beyond the grass and the cyclone fence the big rigs hurtle between Birmingham and Jackson and New Orleans. Sitting by the pool at six o'clock I felt the euphoria of Interstate America: I could be in San Bernardino, or Phoenix, or outside Indianapolis. Children splash in the pool. A three-year-old veers perilously toward the deep end, and her mother calls her back. The mother and her three children are from Georgia, and are staying at the Howard Johnson's while they try to find a new house in Meridian.

"I don't never want to go back to Georgia," the little boy says. "I want this to be my home." "This *will* be your home," the mother says. "Soon as Daddy and I find a house." "I mean this," the little boy says. "This motel."

Another woman appeared and called an older child, a boy twelve or thirteen, in for supper. "We're going to get supper now," she said. "Hell," the boy muttered, and stalked after her wrapped in a Confederate-flag beach towel. The sky darkened, thunder clapped, the three-year-old cried, and we all went inside to the air-conditioned chill. In a half hour or so the rain stopped, and at midnight I could hear the older children splashing in the lighted pool.

Meridian Notes

On the far side of the parking lot at the Howard Johnson's in Meridian is a raw field with a mudhole and a tiny duck house, with ducks. The ducks shake the muddy water from their white feathers.

In Weidmann's Restaurant, paintings are hung for sale: we sat beneath one with a calling card taped beneath it. "Mrs. Walter Albert Green," the card was engraved, and then, in a neat hand, "Dalewood Lake 'Oil' York, Ala. Price $35.00." There was also a painting appalling in its apprehension of human silences, called "In Between," by James A. Harris, $150. During the few days that I was in Meridian the painting and James A. Harris and his life in Meridian began to haunt me, and I tried to call him, but never reached him. He was at the air force base.

Gibson's Discount, ubiquitous. Mercedes-Benz Agency and "Citroën Service," certainly not so. Coca-Cola signs and the Mid-South Business College and Townsend's College of Cosmetology and the Hotel Lamar shut down. I tried to make an appointment with the director of Townsend's Academy of Cosmetology but he said he wasn't interested in any magazines at the present time. We had misunderstood each other, or we had not. I had an appointment with the director, Mrs. Lewis, of the Mid-South Business College, but when I arrived the doors were locked. I stood a while in the cool corridors of the Lamar Building and went downstairs and drank a Coca-Cola and came back, but the doors were still locked. We had misunderstood one another, or we had not.

An Afternoon in Meridian with Stan Torgerson

When I called Stan Torgerson for lunch at his radio station, WQIC, and asked him the best place to lunch, he said Weidmann's, "but it wouldn't win any Holiday Magazine awards." In fact it had, and was not a bad restaurant, but everyone in Mississippi begins on the defensive. "I'll be the biggest man in a green shirt to come through the door," he advised me. He was, at lunch, wary at first. He said he didn't think I knew what I was doing. I agreed. He refused a drink, saying he wasn't in New York City. Stan Torgerson came out of the cold North (Minnesota, I think) and headed to Memphis, where he went into broadcasting. He worked in Miami, and then, for a year, in San Diego, living in La Jolla. He felt ill at ease in La Jolla—his neighbors kept to themselves, had their own interests—and he wanted to get back south. His son had won a football scholarship to Ole Miss. He was worried about his children and drugs in California. "Excuse me," he said, "but I just haven't reached the point where I think pot is a way of life."

When the black radio station in Meridian came up for sale he bought it. He also broadcasts the Ole Miss games, something he began doing when he was in Memphis. "That's right," he said, "I own the ethnic station, WQIC. In its thirteenth year of serving the black community here." He programs gospel and soul, and reaches 180,000 blacks in several Mississippi and Alabama counties, "the thirty-second-largest black market in the country, sixty miles in all directions and forty-three percent of that area is black. We serve a major black market, program soul music and gospel music, but what does that mean? A month ago in *Billboard* there was a survey pointing out that the Top 40–format stations are playing basically soul. Jackson 5 with 'ABC,' 'Turn Back the Hands of Time,' that's Top 40 but it's soul. Once in a while we throw in some blue-eyed soul, like

Dusty Springfield with 'Son of a Preacher Man.'
We don't play rock because our people don't
dig it. We don't play your underground groups
like the Jefferson Airplane . . . We have goodly
reason to believe that ten to fifteen percent of
our audience is white; some of the phone calls
we get in the afternoon for dedications, they're
definitely white voices. We get thirty-six percent of the audience."

He said I was probably wondering why he
came back to Mississippi. "I came because I
dearly love this state. I had a son—he'll be a
senior this fall—playing football at the University of Mississippi."

He pointed out that Meridian was timber
country, hill country. Pulpwood is the backbone
of the agricultural product. He pointed out
how progressive Meridian was: its three new
hospitals. "In most southern cities there is a
much stronger tendency to old-line money . . .
Southern retailers stayed in business privately,
home-owned, until very recently. In most cases
the retailer has just begun to feel the competi-
tion from the chains. There's the greatest business opportunity in the country right here in

the South . . . We don't have a McDonald's in a city of almost fifty thousand people, don't have any of these franchises here yet. You give me one corner of one intersection in Jackson, Mississippi, or you give me the whole ball of wax right here in Meridian, I'd take the whole ball of wax and I'd put a McDonald's on one corner, a Burger Chef on the other, a Shoney's Po' Boy 'cross the street . . ."

His voice kept on, weaving ever higher flights of economic possibility. "There is and *must* be," he said, a "continued turning to the South by industry. The climate is certainly one reason. Another is that the South *wants* industry, and is willing to give a tax advantage to get it. Another, of course, is that there is a relatively low level of unionism in the South. Lockheed assembles tail sections here and ships them to California for assembly . . .

"Atlanta is the magic city for the young around here, across the whole social spectrum . . . The great migration out in the past ten years has been black, they get these glowing letters, and of course they've got relatively liberal welfare programs in some of the northern states . . . No doubt, too, there appears to be greater opportunity in the North."

More on the progressive nature of Meridian: "Our radio station has probably got as fine a list of blue-chip clients as any in town, black or not. We've got all four banks, and anyone in retailing who's interested in doing business with the black—the black's dollar is very important. The minimum wage was probably the most important thing to happen along these lines, and then food stamps were a good deal, I would say they added millions of dollars to our economy.

"We are in a transitional phase. There's a tremendous push to education on the part of young blacks. The schools here are completely integrated. Of course neither you nor I can change the older black, the forty-year-old, his life patterns are settled.

"Ole Miss has its standards to keep up. As more and more blacks get an educational advantage, you'll see blacks at Ole Miss. There's a feeling among some black leaders that because these kids have not had advantages they should get some kind of educational break, but basically what has to happen is the standards have to stay up and the people come up to meet them."

We were driving through town at night, and Stan Torgerson interrupted himself to point out the post office. "There's the post office, the courthouse where the famous Philadelphia trials were held, the trials for the so-called Philadelphia deaths."

"If there were elm trees hanging over the street it would be very midwestern," Stan observed as we drove through the residential district. He pointed out his $29,500 house, a two-story frame, "twenty-eight hundred square feet, with magnolia, dogwood, and pecan trees." He pointed out Poplar Drive, the "Park Avenue of Meridian, Mississippi, all the houses built by the old-line families."

Fervently, he kept reverting to the wholesomeness of life in Meridian. His daughter, who would be a high school senior in the fall, had "her sports, her outdoor activities, her swimming. It's a quiet, pacific type of living, which is one of the reasons I wanted to come back down here. The kids are taught to say 'sir' and 'ma'am.' I know it's very fashionable to poke fun at the South, but I'll pit our slum area any day against the slum areas where the Cubans and Puerto Ricans live in Miami, Florida, and Miami'll lose."

Meridian is the largest city between Jackson and Birmingham, and there is a naval base there which means a great deal to the community. At apartment buildings largely inhabited by the navy there are cars with plates from all over the country.

Some random social observations from Stan Torgerson included: most of the local children go to college within the state, at Ole Miss or Mississippi or Southern Mississippi; the other country club, built with federal money, has a membership which includes "assistant managers of stores and some navy people"; most of the subdivisions in Meridian feature "custom houses." Torgerson paused dramatically, to emphasize the versatility of the new blood in town: "A fabric store."

I asked if some children did not leave, and he allowed that some did. "Nothing here for the kid with an engineering degree. And of

course the girls go where they marry. Southern girls are notoriously husband hunting, but
I guess that's the same anywhere." It occurred
to me almost constantly in the South that had I
lived there I would have been an eccentric and
full of anger, and I wondered what form the
anger would have taken. Would I have taken
up causes, or would I have simply knifed
somebody?

Torgerson was wound up now, and I could
not stop his peroration. "There's been a great
metamorphosis in recent years in the South,
the Volkswagen dealership for example compa-
rable in size to anything you'll find anywhere.

"The KKK which used to be a major factor in this community isn't a factor anymore,
both the membership and the influence have
diminished, and I cannot think of any place
where the black is denied entrance, with the
possible exception of private clubs. We don't
have any antagonistic-type black leaders working against racial harmony. Since the advent
of black pride, black power, there is a little
tendency to be self-segregating. On our station, we have a program we call *Adventures in*

Black History, to point out the contributions
black people have made—a black minister
does it. I have blacks working in the WQIC
Soul Shop, and there's a black druggist here,
a man eminently qualified, who is a local boy
who went north and came back, received his
training at the University of Illinois. We have
a certain degree of black business, includ-
ing this gas station here, which is owned by a
black. The key is racial harmony, and education, and we'll try to provide our people with
both, 'cause we're gonna live together a long
time. Every major retailer hires black clerks,
Sears has a couple of black department heads,
there's a black business college here, and a
black and white Career Training Institute.

"Of course we have transplants, too, new
ideas, like any other hybrid we're generally
stronger. We're not nearly as inbred as we used
to be. We've been withdrawn in this part of the
South for many, many years, but we've become
more aggressive, and as people come in they've
helped us become more aggressive—we don't
wear crinolines anymore, no we don't.

"And about our politics, well, George Wallace got a lot of votes in Indiana, let's face it. I'm not saying I'm going to have a black minister come home to dinner tonight, 'cause I'm not. But things are changing. I had a man the other day, owns an appliance store, he never believed you could send a black repairman into somebody's house. Now he can't find a white . . . He asks me if I know a black man who makes a good appearance. That's progress . . .

"Of course, there's a tremendous lack of skilled blacks, and the problem is training and education. It's no longer a matter of lack of opportunity, it's a matter of lack of skills. We're still two generations from full equality, but so are they in Chicago, in Detroit, and have you ever been in Harlem?"

Glazed by the two hours in which this man in the green shirt had laid Meridian out before us as an entrepreneur's dream, a Shoney's Po' Boy on every corner and progress everywhere, even at the country club, I dropped him off and drove through the still-deserted streets of the downtown. A few black women were on the streets, and they carried umbrellas against the sun. It was almost five o'clock. In the middle of 22nd Avenue, the main street of Meridian, there was a man holding a shotgun. He had on a pink shirt and a golfing cap, and in one ear there was a hearing aid. He raised the shotgun and shot toward the roof of a building several times.

I stopped the car and watched him a while, then approached him. "What are you shooting at?" I asked.

"*Pi-ea*gins," he said cheerfully.

In this one demented afternoon Mississippi lost much of its power to astonish me.

Because I had fallen and hurt a rib in New Orleans, and the rib pained me in the steaming heat and when I swam or turned in bed, I decided to see a doctor in Meridian. I was unsure how long it would be before I was again in a town big enough to have an emergency clinic, and here there were, Stan Torgerson had told me repeatedly, four hospitals, and I even knew the name of one, the Rush Foundation Hospital, and so I went there. One of the younger Rush doctors looked at my rib and sent me for an X-ray. I do not know if it was Dr. Vaughn Rush or Dr. Lowry Rush, who are brothers, or Dr. Gus Rush, who is a cousin. Before the doctor came in a nurse took my history, and she seemed not to believe a word I said. While I waited in my white smock I began to see it through her eyes: A woman walks into a clinic, a stranger to Meridian. She has long straight hair, which is not seen in the South among respectable women past the age of fourteen, and she complains of an injured rib. She gives her address as Los Angeles, but says the rib was injured in a hotel room in New Orleans. She says she is just "traveling through" Meridian. This is not a story to inspire confidence, and I knew it as I told it, which made meeting her eyes difficult.

Dr. Rush himself was willing to let this story go at face value, more or less.

"Just traveling on vacation," he said.

"Actually I'm a writer," I said. "I like going places I've never been."

"Traveling alone?" He pressed at my rib.

"With my husband."

This did not sound exactly right, either, because I was not wearing my wedding ring. There was a long pause.

"I went to school up north," he said. "I liked it a lot up there. I thought once I wouldn't mind living up there."

"But you came back here."

"But . . ." he said, "I came back here."

One evening in Meridian we went to the movies: *Loving* was playing with George Segal and Eva Marie Saint. The audience, what there was of it, gazed at the screen as if the movie were Czech. As it happened I had seen Eva Marie Saint a few weeks before, at dinner at someone's house in Malibu, and the distance between Malibu and this movie house in Meridian seemed limitless. How had I gotten from there to here: there, as always, was the question.

NOTE: Thinking about southern girls I had known in New York, the astonishing way their life in the South remained more vivid to them than anything that was happening to them in the city. Esther Nicol, when told I had been a Tri Delt at Berkeley, sniffed and said that at Ole Miss the Tri Delt house was "mostly Mississippi girls." To Esther, who was from Memphis, this meant something real. Again, remembering having lunch with a girl from Nashville who was working at Condé Nast. She would have to leave in a month, she told me, because home in Nashville the season was beginning and her grandmother was giving a party.

NOTE: On being asked for identification when I ordered a drink in the rural South. Before I came south I had not been taken for seventeen in considerable years, but several times in that month I had to prove I was eighteen. It is assumed that grown women will have their hair done, is all I could think.

NOTE: Remembering that in Durham in 1942 there was something, or was said to be something, called Push Day, when blacks would push whites on the streets. People avoided going downtown shopping on Push Day, which was either Tuesday or Wednesday. And there was that time in Durham, when Mother and my brother, Jimmy, and I got on a bus to go out to Duke and the driver would not start because we were sitting in the back of the bus.

On the Road from Meridian to Tuscaloosa, Alabama

Signs: WELCOME TO ALABAMA! TAKE A FUN BREAK!

782,000 ALABAMA BAPTISTS WELCOME YOU!

Dixie Gas stations, all over, with Confederate flags and grillwork.

Boys working on the road between Cuba and Demopolis. Making measurements with fishing poles. Sumter County, Alabama, around in here, is 80 percent black. We crossed the Demopolis Rooster Bridge over the Tombigbee River, another still, brown river. I think I never saw water that appeared to be running in any part of the South. A sense of water moccasins.

In Demopolis around lunchtime the temperature was 96 degrees and all movement seemed liquid. An Alabama state trooper drove slowly around town. I put a penny in a weighing machine on the main street. My weight was ninety-six, and my fortune was "You are inclined to let your heart rule your head."

In the drugstore a young girl was talking to the woman at the counter. "I'm gonna run off and get married," the girl said. "Who to?" the woman asked. The girl crumpled her straw paper. "I'm gonna get married," she said stubbornly, "I don't care who."

To get out of the sun I sat a while in the Demopolis library and contemplated a newspaper photograph of the Demopolis police force (nine of them) pouring out 214 gallons of confiscated moonshine. The moonshine had been confiscated after a four-hour chase and tracking with a bloodhound. The driver of the moonshine car, Clarence Bunyan Barrett of Cedartown, Georgia, was fined $435 and released.

At the desk a small birdlike woman about seventy was chatting with the librarian.

"*The Nashville Sound* in yet?"

"Still on order," the librarian said.

"How 'bout *The World of Fashion*?"

"Still out."

"Put me down on the waiting list for *The World of Fashion*."

The French Lieutenant's Woman was moving briskly that summer in the Demopolis library. The temperature at two was 98 degrees.

Greene County rolls gently, trees and grass, a light clear green. Pasture. The land looks rich, and many people from Birmingham, etc. (rich people) maintain places here to hunt.

The southern myth: a small bungalow named Grayfield, lots and lots of small one-story houses with two-by-four pillars.

Eutaw, Alabama, is a town the train goes through. Children were bicycling in town, barely moving in the leafy still air. There were tiger lilies everywhere, wild or naturalized. We listened to country music on the radio. There was a funeral taking place at the Eutaw Baptist Church at 4 p.m. on June 16, and the mourners made a frieze outside the church with a group of children on a penny hike. The coin spinning on the sidewalk and the children kneeling to see, with the adults in black around them. In Eutaw there was a white swimming pool and a black swimming pool, and an apartment house, the Colonial Apts., where the sign read APPLY JIMMY'S GRILL.

In the Eutaw City Hall I asked a clerk where the Chamber of Commerce was, but she could not, or would not, tell me. On a corner was a locked-up Teen Center, with posters inside that read GO TIDE and FREAK-OUT. There was one poster of a peace symbol. Children represent a mysterious subculture in small southern towns.

At 5 p.m. on a Tuesday afternoon we drove down a side road into Ralph, Alabama. A sign told us that the ZIP was 35480, the pop. 50, and that the town included:

Bethel (Baptist)
Shiloh (Baptist)
Wesley Chapel
Post Office
School.

Ralph was also a Prize Winner for Cotton Improvement. Tiger lilies and no people, anywhere.

Off US 82-W, near Tuscaloosa, is Lake Lurleen. Bear Bryant Volkswagen in Tuscaloosa. Rebel Oil. Bumper stickers: "Yahweh vs. Evolution / Don't Make a Monkey Out of Yourself." Tiger Lilies. Red Tide, Crimson Tide, Go Tide, Roll Tide.

At the Ramada Inn in Tuscaloosa I sat outside by the swimming pool about five o'clock one afternoon and read Sally Kempton's piece in *Esquire* about her father and other men she had known. There was no sun. The air was as liquid as the pool. Everything seemed to be made of concrete, and damp. A couple of men in short-sleeved nylon shirts sat at another metal table and drank beer from cans. Later we tried to find somewhere open to eat. I called a place on University Boulevard, and the owner said to turn left at the Skyline Drive-in. On the way we got lost and stopped in a gas station to ask directions. The attendant had no idea where University Boulevard was (the University of Alabama is on University Boulevard) but could give us directions to the Skyline.

Birmingham

When I called a friend in Birmingham to ask who I should see around the countryside, what was going on, and he asked me what I wanted to know and I explained, he said, "You want to see who's sitting around the Greyhound bus station and who's sitting around in a Packard car, is that right?" I said that was right.

The country way in which he gave me names: "There's ole Rankin Fife, Speaker of the state House of Representatives, he pretty much runs Winfield. Over to Boligee there's David Johnston, he's got a big farm. There's a union leader, the Haneys, they live outside Guin, and he's a farmer and a preacher and a union leader. There's the Hill family, they run the bank. There's Boyd Aman in Boligee, number one hunter and fisherman—I reckon you could find him at the general store. And if you get in any trouble up there, you be sure to call me."

The sense of sports being the opiate of the people. In all the small towns the high school gymnasium was not only the most resplendent part of the high school but often the most solid structure in the town, redbrick, immense, a monument to the hopes of the citizenry. Athletes who were signing "letters of intent" were a theme in the local news.

At dinner one night in Birmingham there were, besides us, five people. Two of the men had gone to Princeton and the third was, when he was traveling on business, a habitué of Elaine's in New York and the Beverly Hills Hotel in California. They talked with raucous good humor about "seein' those X-rated movies" when their wives were out of town. This was a manner of speaking, a rococo denial of their own sophistication, which I found dizzying to contemplate.

"You could almost say that all the virtues and all the limitations of the South are a function of low population," someone said at lunch in Birmingham. "Cities, well, cities *are* melting pots. What we've had here was an almost feudal situation." We had been in places in

Mississippi and Alabama where there had been virtually no ethnic infusion.

"Leave 'em to their stamps," someone said at dinner about the white tenants on his father's place.

Southern houses and buildings once had space and windows and deep porches. This was perhaps the most beautiful and comfortable ordinary architecture in the United States, but it is no longer built, because of air-conditioning.

NOTE: The curious ambivalence of the constant talk about wanting industry. Is not wanting industry the death wish, or is wanting it?

Talking about "a gentleman of the old school," there was the familiarity with generations of eccentric behavior, scandals and arrangements, high extramarital drama played out against the Legion parade.

It is said that the dead center of Birmingham society is the southeast corner of the locker room at the Mountain Brook country club. At Mountain Brook everyone goes to St. Luke's Episcopal Church or Briarwood Presbyterian, and it is hard to make the connection between this Birmingham and that of Bull Connor, and Birmingham Sunday.

Lunch with Hugh Bailey at the club, up high enough to see the smoke haze. "We got a pollution count in Birmingham now, which I guess you could say is a sign of progress." On that day the *Birmingham Post-Herald* (June 18) reported the downtown pollution count at 205, or over the U.S. Public Health Service's critical level, and the number of respiratory deaths in Jefferson County that week at six. There did not seem to be much pollution in Mountain Brook.

In Birmingham at dinner they were talking about catching rattlesnakes. "You take a hose, and go out in the fields, and take a few drops of gasoline down the hose into a hole—any hole—and that makes the rattlesnakes kind of drunk, and they come out for some air."

At every social level, the whole quality of maleness, the concentration on hunting and fishing. Leave the women to their cooking, their canning, their "prettifying."

A sign in a trailer camp in Walker County, Alabama: YOUR VOTE AND SUPPORT APPRECIATED/WALLACE FOR GOVERNOR. The thought that the reason Wallace has never troubled me is that he is a totally explicable phenomenon.

Most southerners are political realists: they understand and accept the realities of working politics in a way we never did in California. Graft as a way of life is accepted, even on the surface. "You get somebody makes eight hundred dollars a month as state finance director, he's only got four years to make his stake."

Inscriptions on gravestones:

THE ANGELS CALLED HIM

DYING IS BUT GOING HOME

MOORE

ELLIE   JESSIE T.

1888–19   1887–1952

SANDLIN

RAND   IDA M.
1871–1952   1873–19

JENNIE B., *wife of J. R. Jones.*
She was a kind and affectionate wife,
a fond aunt, and a friend to all.

In so many family plots there was someone
recently dead—dead after World War II—
who remembered the Civil War. This was in a
graveyard in a harsh red-dirt hill town, plastic flowers on the plots, overlooking the bright
lights of the ballpark.

At the St. Francis Motel in Birmingham I
went swimming, which occasioned great notice
in the bar. "Hey, look, there's somebody with
a bikini on."

Winfield

Maybe the rural South is the last place in America where one is still aware of trains and what they can mean, their awesome possibilities.

I put my clothes in the laundromat and walked on down the dirt at the side of the road to the beauty shop. A girl with long straight blond hair gave me a manicure. Her name was Debby.

"I got one more year at Winfield High," Debby said, "then I'm getting out."

I asked her where she would get out to.

"Birmingham," she said.

I asked what she would do in Birmingham.

"Well, if I keep on working while I'm in school, I'll have enough hours for my cosmetologist's license. You need three thousand, I got twelve hundred already. Then I'll go to modeling school." Debby reflected a moment. "I hope I will."

An electric fan hummed in the small shop. The smell of hair conditioners, shampoos, warm and sticky. The only other person there was the daughter of the proprietress. I asked her if she was still in school. She giggled as if she did not believe anyone could ask such a silly question.

"I been *married* three years," she said.

"You don't look old enough," I said.

"I'm *twenty.*"

She lives in a trailer with her husband, Scott, who operates a power saw. Trailers got hot, we all agreed. They cool down at night, Debby suggested. "Oh, sure," the twenty-year-old said, "it cools down at night." Her mother, who owned the beauty shop, was home "doing her bookwork." She was in charge, and bossing Debby slightly. "You didn't get her *name*? She couldn't come any other *time*?"

They revert to the theme of the heat. The trailer does cool down at night, they agreed.

"Last night it was cool," the twenty-year-old said.

"I didn't think so," Debby said.

"I don't mean when we went to *bed*, I mean late. I woke up, it was almost cool. 'Course I'd had the *conditioning* on in the trailer all day."

Debby looked impassively out the open door. "So hot, Daddy had to come out from the bedroom to sleep on the couch."

"Cooler in than out."

Debby dried my hands. "I guess," she said idly.

At the little concrete pool between the motel and the creek, two teenage girls in two-piece bathing suits were lying in the sun on the stained pavement. They had come in a pickup truck and a transistor radio on the seat of the pickup played softly. There was algae in the pool, and a cigarette butt. "ABC," the Jackson 5.

I bought a large paper cup full of cracked ice in the drugstore (Hollis Pharmacy) for a nickel and walked back down the road to the laundromat eating it. Nothing had changed in the laundromat in the hour or so I had been gone: the same women, most with rollers in their hair, sat and stared and folded frayed flower-printed towels and sheets. There were two men in the laundromat, a repairman and an officious young man, straw-haired and rednecked, who seemed to be the owner. He regarded the women with contempt and the women regarded him in sullen impassivity.

"Hot 'nough for you?" a middle-aged woman said to me. I said it was. There was no hostility toward or even curiosity about me in the laundromat: by virtue of spending a summer afternoon in this steaming bleak structure I had moved into a realm where all women are sisters in misery. "Use this one," the woman said a while later, pointing out a dryer to me. "This one's dried her clothes and mine both, and she just put in one dime." The woman glanced furtively at the repairman as she spoke, and at the owner, as if fearful that they might fix the machine, deprive us of our jackpot.

On weekday afternoons in towns like Winfield one sees mainly women, moving like somnambulists through the days of their lives.

The men work out at plants somewhere, or on farms, or in lumber. When I left the laundromat there was a boy in a bike helmet working on the road. Bike helmets had come to seem a normal mode of dress. *How the West Was Won* was playing at the movie house.

In the Angelyn Restaurant in Winfield at lunchtime a number of men, among the few I saw in town in the daytime, sat around and watched *General Hospital* on the television.

Guin

A traveler in the rural South in the summertime is always eating dinner, dispiritedly, in the barely waning heat of the day. One is a few hundred miles and a culture removed from any place that serves past 7:30 or 8 p.m. We ate dinner one night at a motel on the road between Winfield and Guin. The sun still blazed on the pavement outside, and was filtered only slightly by the aqueous blue-green Pliofilm shades on the windows inside. The food seemed to have been deep-fried for the lunch business and kept lukewarm on a steam table. Eating is an ordeal, as in an institution, something to be endured in the interests of survival. There are no drinks to soften the harshness of it. Ice is begrudged. I remember in one such place asking for iced coffee. The waitress asked me how to make it. "Same way as iced tea," I said. She looked at me without expression. "In a cup?" she asked.

The waitress in the place in Guin trailed me to the cash register. She was holding a matchbook I had left on the table. "I was looking at your matchbook," she said. "Where's it from?" I said it was from Biloxi. "Biloxi, *Mississippi*?" she said, and studied the matchbook as if it were a souvenir from Nepal. I said yes. She tucked the matchbook in her pocket and turned away.

On the outskirts of Guin the sign says GU-WIN/CITY LIMIT. At the Wit's Inn in Guin, an MYF (I think) coffeehouse, there were a couple of kids with guitars entertaining. They were billed as Kent and Phil, and their last engagement had been at Tuscaloosa. They sang "Abraham, Martin and John" and "Bridge over Troubled Water," and the children in the place joined in when asked, in clear sweet voices.

Some of the boys were wearing Guin baseball uniforms and one beautiful boy about sixteen was wearing a tie-dyed shirt and pants. Kids would drink Cokes and then drift out to the street and talk to somebody idling by in a car and then drift back in. The night was warm and there was fresh corn growing high along the road just past town. It seemed a good and hopeful place to live, and yet the pretty girls, if they stayed around Guin, would end up in the laundromat in Winfield, or in a trailer with the air-conditioning on all night.

When the program ended about ten kids all stood around in the street, making idle connections. A half an hour later the only people seen on the streets of Guin were twelve-year-olds wearing baseball uniforms. We drove between Guin and Hamilton on the George C. Wallace White Way, four lanes to nowhere, brightly lit.

In Hamilton the street lights were turned off. We were getting Fort Worth and San Antonio on the car radio, gospel stations, "Rock of Ages" and "Lonesome Valley." Drove into a drive-in to see the end of *The Road Hustlers,* starring Jim Davis, Andy Devine, and Scott Brady. *The Losers* was the next bill at the drive-in. We followed *The Losers* all over the South. Outside Guin the night shift was working at the 3M plant.

Grenada, Mississippi

Driving over from Oxford to Grenada to have dinner one night with Bob Evans, Jr., and his wife, I noticed the shadows on the kudzu vine, the vine consuming trees, poles, everything in its range. The kudzu makes much of Mississippi seem an ominously topiary landscape. And the graveyards everywhere, with plastic sweet peas on the graves of infants. Death is still natural and ever present in the South, as it is no more in those urbanized parts of the country where graveyards are burial parks and relegated to unused or unusable land far from sight.

On Highway 7, Buck Brown & Son filling station. The rifles slung across the back cab windows of pickups. The Yalobusha Country Club just south of Water Valley. In Water Valley, blacks hanging around the main street, the highway, leaning on cars, talking across the street, the highway. In Coffeeville, Miss., at 6 p.m., there was a golden light and a child swinging in it, swinging from a big tree, over a big lawn, back and forth in front of a big airy house. To be a white middle-class child in a small southern town must be on certain levels the most golden way for a child to live in the United States.

On Margin Street in Grenada, as we drove in, a girl in a yellow bridesmaid's dress and a tulle headpiece, her husband in a cutaway, walked home from a wedding carrying their daughter, a baby two or three.

At the Evanses' house, there was a framed

Christmas card from The President and Mrs. Nixon, and what appeared to be a framed slave deed. We had drinks, and after a while we took our drinks, our road glasses, and went for a drive through town. Mrs. Evans had grown up in Grenada, had been married once before, and now she and her second husband—who was from Tupelo—lived in her mother's old house. "Look at all those people standing around in front of that motel," she said once on the drive. "That's a cathouse," her husband told her. We went out to a lake, and then to dinner at the Holiday Inn, this being another of those towns where the Holiday Inn was the best place to eat. We brought our drinks and a bottle in with us, because there was no liquor served, only setups. I am unsure whether the bottle was legal. The legality or illegality of liquor in the South seems a complication to outsiders, but is scarcely considered by the residents. At dinner some people were watching us, and later came over to say hello to the Evanses. They introduced us as friends from California. "We were wondering where you were from," one of them said.

. . .

On our drive we passed a five-year-old in base-ball pajamas playing catch with a black maid in a white uniform, the ball going back and forth, back and forth, suspended in amber.

The Evanses had a little baby, their child, and a sixteen-year-old daughter, her child. "She only comes out of her room when it's time to eat or time to go out," he said about her.

About the bottle at dinner: actually we brought three bottles, Scotch, bourbon, and vodka, and it was not legal to bring them inside in this dry county, because Mrs. Evans had them in a large handbag she carried exactly for this purpose.

About the cathouse: the notion that an accepted element in the social order is a whorehouse goes hand in hand with the woman on a pedestal.

Oxford

In the student union at Ole Miss they were watching *General Hospital* on the TV, just as they had been in the Angelyn Restaurant in Winfield.

In the student union there was an official calendar for May, on which was printed "May 28—Vacation—Raise Hell." Below this someone had scribbled, "An appropriate preoccupation for an Ole Miss student." The self-image of the Southern Blood as Cavalier very apparent here.

In the university bookstore, which appeared to be the one place in Oxford to buy a book (with the exception of a drugstore on the square which had several racks of paperbacks), the only books available other than assigned texts were a handful of popular bestsellers and a few (by no means all) novels by William Faulkner.

At the swimming pool at the Holiday Inn, the musical dialogue:

"Get that penny, it's down there yonder."

"Hurt my toe."

"I hurt *my* toe climbing a plum tree."

"*How'd* you hurt your toe?"

"Climbed a plum tree."

"Why."

"Get a plum."

"Hey, Bruiser, drop my sneaks down?"

"OK, Goose."

In the parking lot at the Holiday Inn one afternoon a police car was parked, its door open, the police radio breaking the still afternoon air the whole time I was sitting by the pool. Later when I was swimming a little girl pointed out to me that by staying underwater one could hear, by some electronic freak, a radio playing. I submerged and heard news of the Conservative victory in Great Britain, and "Mrs. Robinson."

When I was driving in the afternoon alone on the Ole Miss campus the wind came up, sudden and violent, and the sky darkened and there was thunder but no rain. I was afraid of a tornado. The suddenness and unpredictability of this shocked me. The weather around here must shape ideas of who and what one is, as it does everywhere.

On the same afternoon I saw a black girl on the campus: she was wearing an Afro and a clinging jersey, and she was quite beautiful, with a NY-LA coastal arrogance. I could not think what she was doing at Ole Miss, or what she thought about it.

At dinner in the Holiday Inn, overhearing an academic foursome: two teachers, the wife of one of them, and a younger woman, perhaps a graduate student or a teaching assistant. They were talking about how the SAEs and the Sigma Nus and the Sigma Chis used to "control politics." The break in this situation had come when Archie Manning, who was I believe a Sigma Nu, had run for something and either lost, or just barely won, which went to prove. There had been "a little article in the *Mississippian* about this," about the way the Greeks used to run things, and, said one of the men, "it said they did no more, but it upset my wife and daughter. Why did that have to be?"

The others added that the piece had been "trivial," "not very well done," but they did not address themselves to their colleague's plaintive question.

At one point during dinner the younger woman stated in a spirit of reckless defiance, "I don't care what the student union looks like, I couldn't care less." At another point she said that she believed the FBI had her "staked out," because she had two friends who used drugs. She did not and would not use drugs herself, she added: "My mind's expanded enough."

When I think about Oxford now I think about Archie Manning, the Sigma Nu, and all the bumper stickers that read ARCHIE and ARCHIE'S ARMY, with a Rebel flag, and about the immense and beautifully landscaped fraternity and sorority houses that surround the campus, and about boys and girls who in 1970 come out of the pinewoods to sing "White Star of Sigma Nu" at dances after football games. I had telephoned someone I knew in the English Department at Berkeley to ask if he knew any-

one on any faculty in any department at any
college in Mississippi to whom I should talk,
anyone noted in any field he knew about, but
he did not, and could only suggest that I call
up Miss Eudora Welty, in Jackson.

As a matter of fact I had intended to, if ever
I got near Jackson, but I was afraid to get too
near Jackson because planes left from Jackson for New York and California, and I knew I
would not last ten minutes in Jackson without
telephoning Delta or National and getting out.
All that month I hummed in my mind "Leavin'
on a Jet Plane," Peter, Paul and Mary, and
every night in our motel room we got out the
maps and figured out how many hours' driving
time to Jackson, to New Orleans, to Baton
Rouge, to the closest place the planes left from.

We drove out on Old Taylor Road at night
to look for Rowan Oak, William Faulkner's
house. There were fireflies, and heat lightning,
and the thick vines all around, and we could
not see the house until the next day. It was
large and private, secluded, set back from the
road. I read a book about Faulkner in Oxford,
interviews with his fellow citizens in Oxford,

and I was deeply affected by their hostility to him and by the manner in which he had managed to ignore it. I thought if I took a rubbing from his gravestone, a memento from this place, I would know every time I looked at it that the opinion of others counted for not much one way or another.

So we went out to the graveyard, the Oxford cemetery, to look for the grave. Under a live oak tree a black kid sat in a parked two-tone salmon Buick, the door open. He was sitting on the floorboard with his feet outside, and while I was there several cars with Ole Miss and Archie's Army stickers came winding up the cemetery road, and boys would get out, and they would have some dealing with the black kid and drive away. He seemed to be dealing marijuana, and his car had a Wayne State sticker. Other than that there was nobody, just rabbits and the squirrels and the hum of bees and the heat, dizzying heat, heat so intense I thought of fainting. For several hours we looked for the grave, found the Faulkner plot and a number of other Faulkner/Falkner graves, but we never found William Faulkner's grave, not in that whole graveyard full of Oxford citizens and infant sons.

The way in which all the reporting tricks I had ever known atrophied in the South. There were things I should do, I knew it: but I never did them. I never made an appointment with the bridal consultant of the biggest department store in any town I was in. I never made the Miss Mississippi Hospitality Contest Semi-Finals, although they were being held in little towns not far from where we were, wherever we were. I neglected to call the people whose names I had, and hung around drugstores instead. I was underwater in some real sense, the whole month.

I kept talking to Mrs. Frances Kirby by telephone in Jackson. Mrs. Kirby was in charge of the Miss Hospitality contests, in Bay Springs, Cleveland, Clinton, Greenwood, Gulfport, Indianola, Leland, Lewisville. I was within a few miles of Cleveland on the day that contest would be held, and I called the sponsors, the chamber of commerce, and they said to come on "up at the country club" and watch, but I never even did that.

A Sunday Lunch in Clarksdale

One day we drove from Oxford over to Clarksdale, to have Sunday lunch with Marshall Bouldin and his wife, Mel. Lunch was served promptly at noon, a few minutes after our arrival. There was fried chicken and gravy, white rice, fresh green peas, and a peach pie for dessert. The heat was so intense that the ice was already melted in the Waterford water goblets before we sat down at the table. Grace was said. The children were allowed to speak on topics of interest, but not to interrupt. I have never eaten so long or heavy a meal. I was in a place where "Sunday" still existed as it did in my grandmother's house, a leadening pause in the week, a day of boredom so extreme as to be

exhausting. It was the kind of Sunday to make
one ache for Monday morning.

After lunch we sat in the living room of the
small house in town the Bouldins were using
while their plantation house was being remodeled. Marshall Bouldin talked, and here are
some of the things he said:

"The money and the power in the South have
traditionally been in the hands of the people
who plant. The Delta, because of that, is rich.
There are rich people in the Delta. You don't
get governors from the Delta, but you do get
the money and the power to elect them. Governors come from the hills, and from Hattiesburg. There's a lieutenant governor now from
Clarksdale, but that's unusual. There are fewer
blacks in the hill sections. The Delta, which
is more affluent, has a higher black population. The third part of Mississippi, besides the
hills and the Delta, is the coastal area, which
is really an isolated phenomenon.

"I'm so glad to see what has happened in
Mississippi. The thinking has come so far in
just these twenty years. The hill country is certainly more reactionary. The Delta's still con-

servative, yes, but people here have money, and people who have money can be exposed to new ideas.

"Mainly we plant cotton here, soybeans are replacing truck crops. We tried cattle, but the soil here is too rich for cattle, the flat land ends at Vicksburg. The Delta is maybe fifty miles wide, and was all overflow land until after the Civil War when the levees were built. Around 1870, then, people began to move in, they had this rich land, all river silt. What size is the average Delta farm? Well, fourteen thousand acres would be a large one, and two hundred to three hundred acres would be a small one, the average is said to be seven hundred seventy, but that would be small for cotton or beans.

"Thirty years ago my dad and my Mel's dad led the ideal planter's life. Now it's more of a business, it's not the same. It was a series of small towns then, there were great social functions, and you went from town to town for your social functions, and this held the country together.

"What you have here is the last of the feudal system. It's an area where you have plenty of

servants. We're fortunate to have Charles and
Frances here, they were on my dad's place.
What you had around here until very lately
was mainly the tenant system. Each black family was responsible for the ten or fifteen acres
around his cabin. The owner supervised and
provided food, and provided anything else the
family needed, and these were sizable families, but they'd say, 'Mr. Marshall, take care of
me,' and we would. That's part of the change
here. Mel's brother is not on the tenant system.

"My dad never put anyone off. And Mel,
your dad never did either. Some planters,
they abused the tenant system. There was
one planter around here, on payday he used
to make them smile, he'd hand out silver dollars when he got the smile, but that was just
some, and maybe it was condoned but it was
never approved of. Mel's daddy kept *books*,
and settled with every tenant. The community knew who these people were who took
advantage, and frowned on them. Of course,
nobody put them in jail, which is maybe what
we should've done.

"Automation changed things, the cotton

picker meant we didn't need so many. We
never put anybody off the land, they just grad-
ually left for Detroit or they moved into town.
A few planters told people to get off, but on the
whole there was not much dispossessing of the
black man.

"The big change, I do think, was when television came. The kids could see the way other
people lived, other lives. It has been the greatest educational system in the county.

"My dad's main job was just talking to John,
seeing if he needed anything (John was the
overseer or foreman). Mel's brother, on the
other hand, he runs—I don't want to say it's
a factory, but it turns out cotton. He has about
three thousand acres in three pieces. In 1950 I
farmed like my daddy farmed, on a horse. Now
you need to have a manager on each place, in
his pickup. You need to have a personal radio,
to be able to reach a man you've got in town
and tell him to get that part out here in fifteen
minutes. You used to be able to have a good
time farming. When you got the cotton picked
in the fall you read books, went hunting, sat
around the fire and socialized. Now, they're

working on the machinery all winter. Maybe if you can get the repair work done in January, you can take a month or six weeks off in February, but that's it." He paused, and looked at his wife. "Isn't that right, Mel?"

Mel shrugged. "It's still the good life," she said.

"The black population is still high here," he went on. "In the schools right now it's 80 percent black and 20 percent white, now that we're integrated. We have tortured and tortured over what to do with our children, and our tentative decision for now is to send them to private schools, even though that is against our ideals. I can't sacrifice my child to my ideal. They had to force the black to integrate. Basically I know that the people who are pushing it are right, but they seem so precipitous. They say we had to integrate on February 2. Now, why couldn't they have waited 'til September? It hardened attitudes, is what it did. There are people in this community who might have been showing signs of opening up their minds, and then a parent finds out that as of next week his kid is going to be over in Higgins High—that door is closed, and when it's going to open again nobody knows.

"They say around here it takes three generations to make a gentleman, and yet if I was about a sixteen-year-old black boy I'll be damned if I'd want to wait three generations. All over this area we still have these large maternal families, families with no daddy, nobody to say if you're going to reap the benefits, you've got to put in the work.

"I'm a middle-of-the-roader, and like the majority, we're trying to do the easiest thing that will get us all by happily. There are five or six houses in Clarksdale right now where this conversation could take place. That may not seem like many but when I was growing up there were none.

"The best thing we can do is raise our children differently, and add four people to the community who can come home from this little Episcopal school and think differently. When the integration orders were flying around Mississippi last year it was hard to think what to do, and it still is."

Charles and Frances came out from the

kitchen, to say goodbye. They were on their way to church. Marshall Bouldin beamed as he introduced them. "Charles and Frances were on my daddy's place, isn't that right, Frances?" Frances bobbed her head. "That's right, surely is," she said. "Mr. Marshall and us, we were little itty-bittys together."

There was news of a tornado somewhere near the Delta, although not in Coahoma County, and a telephone call to inform Marshall Bouldin that "a black man died on the place last night."

We drove out to the plantation, where the house was being remodeled. He pointed out the tenant cabins standing empty. "When I was little we farmed it all with mules," he said. "When I went off to college we had four-row equipment. Now we have six-row equipment." He pointed out the tractors, which cost $15,000 apiece, and added that there were $60,000 worth of tractors alone in the shed. He pointed out what had been his father's payoff office, and one tenant cabin which was occupied. "This is one of the tenant cabins still occupied by my old fishing buddy, Ernie." Ernie calls the Bouldins Miss Mel and Mister Marshall.

"That's cotton," he said, "far back as the cypress break." I asked what was beyond the cypress break. "Some more of our place."

Mel Bouldin, for a southern woman of her age and class, had done an extraordinary thing: she had gone to medical school after the birth of her children, and now practiced ob-gyn in Memphis, in partnership with three men. She flew to Memphis from "the place" in a private plane. "I can't stand to sit around the country club and *talk*," she said by way of explanation.

She was, at the time we visited her, taking a year off her practice to supervise the reconstruction of the house. The house was to be "a boys' house, everything rough and ready." "I love boys," she kept saying. In certain ways she seemed to have been affected by the great leap she had taken out of her time and place: in order to be her own woman she had found it necessary to vehemently reject many of the things which traditionally give women pleasure, cooking ("'Course I hate to cook, I'd walk a mile and a half to avoid it"), any vanity about her own appearance, any interest in having her house reflect her own tastes. Her mother's house reflected her mother: Mel's house would reflect "the boys," and her greatest delight was in secret stairways and hideaways she was having built into the walls for the children.

At lunch, or just before, the seven-year-old had been asked to perform, and did so with pleasure, playing "Joy to the World" on the piano, a peculiar melody on this steaming June day in the Delta. Everyone held hands during the blessing at table. The four boys were dressed in matching blue mandarin shirts. The family had just come from church services, at the Presbyterian church. When I called the day before from Oxford and Marshall Bouldin suggested we come to lunch, he had said, "Come after church." The idea of "church" as a Sunday morning donnée has not existed for a couple of generations in the Protestant societies I know, but it exists in the South.

On our drive, we passed Delta Road, where there live "nothing but blacks, or if there were any whites, I wouldn't want to meet them."

Out behind the house, the immense Sears, Roebuck swimming tank, raised five or six feet above the lawn. "Keeps the snakes and frogs out," Mel said.

Clarksdale calls itself "The Golden Buckle on the Cotton Belt." At parties in the Delta they say to one another: "How yo' cotton coming?" And then: "Yeah? What's wrong?"

On Silk Stocking Row in Clarksdale there live a few planters, a lawyer, and the cotton broker. Many of the planters live in town. There is one plantation around Clarksdale owned by an English syndicate.

Down the Delta to Greenville

Outside the Bolivar County Courthouse in Rosedale, an old policeman, his collar loosened around his thick neck, sat in his car with the motor idling in the Sunday twilight.

Outside Rosedale, on the sign for a RR crossing, the letters KKK had been painted.

All the billboards were for cotton and soybean insecticides and fertilizers.

In Benoit, the town where *Baby Doll* was

shot, people hanging around with that remark-
able "vacant" look which people in the South
always mention before you do and then become
defensive about. ("Ever look on a subway in
Detroit, Michigan?")

The endless green of the Delta, the flatness,
the haze in the mornings. The algae-covered
ditches alive with mosquitoes.

In Greenville, the presence of the levee, a
high wall at the end of every street downtown.
We ate dinner out on the pier at a place that
had good gumbo, and I was glad to be on the
river (actually we were on a slough), glad to be
in a place with good food, glad to be, I suppose,
so very close to the place where the National
and Delta flights left for California.

We went to have dinner with Hodding Carter III and his wife, Peggy, and with Lew Pow-
ell, the city editor of the paper, and his girl.
Hodding picked us up and there was the ubiquitous glass on the dashboard, the road glass,
in this instance a martini.

We went to dinner at Boyt's, a roadhouse
in the next crossroads over. On Boyt's menu:
"Italian or Wop Salad."

Hodding Carter III: "The blacks who leave the Delta say they'd come back if there were just something here—this is a place with a strong pull."

He spoke about New Orleans as the place you cop out to, "you go down there with the eleven-and-a-half-month debutante season." His wife came from New Orleans, went to Miss McGehee's and to Sophie Newcomb, and now, he implied, she lives on the frontier.

It would be a while, he thought, before automation came to southern agriculture. Its arrival in California was "speeded up by labor problems." He saw an industrial New South as a kind of pipe dream, the difficulty being an unskilled labor force. "They talk about cheap labor in the South, but cheap labor is a myth for a national company, for any company with labor contracts. So that's no advantage, and another disadvantage here for industry, we've got social problems you don't have in the North."

"The FBI" as a leitmotif in the South. I had heard it in Biloxi, in Oxford, in Grenada, in Greenville.

The time warp: the Civil War was yesterday, but 1960 is spoken of as if it were about three hundred years ago.

Downriver and Home

The names of plantations going south on 61: Baconia, Lydia, and Evanna. On the billboards: PESTICIDE DYANAP. A plantation south of Onward: Reality Plantation. The Yazoo County Bookmobile, a cropduster releasing sprays of yellow haze. A Greyhound bus with CHICAGO emblazoned over the window hurtling north on 61 through Warren County.

Outside Vicksburg is a shopping center, with a mall named Battlefield Village. In Port Gibson there is a Presbyterian church with, instead of a cross on top of the steeple, a gold finger, pointing heavenward. The kudzu.

Fayette had the aspect of a set from *Porgy and Bess,* in that there were only blacks to be seen on the street and behind windows. The only white I saw as we drove through was wearing a blue work shirt and had a Zapata mustache.

"The Interstate" as a phrase, and a concept. The great pulsing links between there and everywhere else.

On the window of a coffee shop in South McComb, SUPPORT YOUR CITIZEN'S COUNCIL and STATES RIGHTS — RACIAL INTEGRITY, which pretty much laid it right where it was. (Actually I think the restaurant— Boyt's—with Wop Salad on the menu was in McComb, not in Greenville.)

We stopped at Walker Percy's in Covington, Louisiana. We sat out in back by the bayou and drank gin and tonics and when a light rain began to fall, a kind of mist, Walker never paid any mind but just kept talking, and walking up to the house to get fresh drinks. It was a thunderstorm, with odd light, and there were occasional water-skiers on the black bayou water. "The South," he said, "owes a debt to the North . . . tore the Union apart once . . . and now only the South can save the North."

He said he had not wanted to see us in New Orleans, at Ben C.'s, because at Ben C.'s he was always saying things he would not ordinarily say, playing a role. Greenville, he said, was a different kind of town. He had spent some time in Los Angeles once but could not face it. "It was the weather," his wife said mildly. "The weather was bad." "It wasn't the weather," he said, and he knew exactly what it was.

Crossing the Pontchartrain bridge, the gray water, the gray causeway, the gray skyline becoming apparent in the far distance just about the time you lose sight of the shore behind you. The sight of New Orleans coming up like a mirage from about the midway point on the Lake Pontchartrain Causeway.

Sycamores and pit vipers. From Audubon, 1830:

> Deep morasses, overshadowed by millions of gigantic dark cypresses, spreading their sturdy moss-covered branches ... Would that I could represent to you the dangerous nature of the ground, its oozing, spongy, and miry disposition ...

A senseless disagreement on the causeway, ugly words and then silence. We spent a silent night in an airport motel and took the 9:15 National flight to San Francisco. I never wrote the piece.

California Notes

I had told Jann Wenner of Rolling Stone *that I would cover the Patty Hearst trial, and this pushed me into examining my thoughts about California. Some of my notes from the time follow here. I never wrote the piece about the Hearst trial, but I went to San Francisco in 1976 while it was going on and tried to report it. And I got quite involved in uncovering my own mixed emotions. This didn't lead to my writing the piece, but eventually it led to—years later—*Where I Was From *(2003).*

When I was there for the trial, I stayed at the Mark. And from the Mark, you could look into the Hearst apartment. So I would sit in my room and imagine Patty Hearst listening to Carousel. *I had read that she would sit in her room and listen to it. I thought the trial had some meaning for me—because I was from California. This didn't turn out to be true.*

The first time I was ever on an airplane was in 1955, and flights had names. This one was *The Golden Gate*, American Airlines. Serving Transcontinental Travelers Between San Francisco and New York. A week before, twenty-one years old, I had been moping around Berkeley in my sneakers and green raincoat, and now I was a Transcontinental Traveler, Lunching Aloft on Beltsville Roast Turkey with Dressing and Giblet Sauce. I believed in Dark Cottons. I believed in Small Hats and White Gloves. I believed that Transcontinental Travelers did not wear white shoes in the City. The next summer I went back on *The New Yorker*, United Airlines, and had a Martini-on-the-Rocks and Stuffed Celery au Roquefort over the Rockies.

The image of the Golden Gate is very strong in my mind. As unifying images go, this one is particularly vivid.

At the *Sacramento Union* I learned that Eldorado County and Eldorado City are so spelled but that regular usage of El Dorado is two words; to UPPERCASE Camellia Week, the Central Valley, Sacramento Irrigation District, Liberator bombers and Superfortresses, the Follies Bergere [*sic*], the Central Valley Project, and "such nicknames as Death Row, Krauts or Jerries for Germans, Doughboys, Leathernecks, Devildogs."

Arden School class prophecy:

In Carnegie Hall we find Shirley Long
Up on the stage singing a song.
Acting in pictures is Arthur Raney's job,
And he is often followed by a great mob.
As a model Yavette Smith has achieved fame,
Using "Bubbles" as her nickname . . .
We find Janet Haight working hard as a
*   missionary,*
Smart she is and uses a dictionary . . .
We find Joan Didion as a White House
*   resident*
Now being the first woman president.

Looking through the evidence I find what seems to me now (or rather seemed to me then) an entirely spurious aura of social success and achievement. I seem to have gotten my name in the paper rather a lot. I seem to have belonged to what were in context the "right" clubs. I seem to have been rewarded, out of all proportion to my generally undistinguished academic record, with an incommensurate number of prizes and scholarships (merit scholarships only: I did not qualify for need) and recommendations and special attention and very probably the envy and admiration of at least certain of my peers. Curiously, I only remember failing, failures and slights and refusals.

I seem to have gone to dances and been photographed in pretty dresses, and also as a pom-pom girl. I seem to have been a bridesmaid rather a lot. I seem always to have been "the editor" or "the president."

I believed that I would always go to teas.

This is not about Patricia Hearst. It is about me and the peculiar vacuum in which I grew up, a vacuum in which the Hearsts could be quite literally king of the hill.

I have never known deprivation.

"How High the Moon," Les Paul and Mary Ford. *High Noon.*

.   .   .

I have lived most of my life under misapprehensions of one kind or another. Until I was in college I believed that my father was "poor," that we had no money, that pennies mattered. I recall being surprised the first time my small brother ordered a dime rather than a nickel ice cream cone and no one seemed to mind.

My grandmother, who was in fact poor, spent money: the Lilly Daché and Mr. John hats, the vicuña coats, the hand-milled soap and the $60-an-ounce perfume were to her the necessities of life. When I was about to be sixteen she asked me what I wanted for my birthday and I made up a list (an Ultra-Violet lipstick, some other things), meaning for her to pick one item and surprise me: she bought the list. She gave me my first grown-up dress, a silk jersey dress printed with pale blue flowers and jersey petals around the neckline. It came from the Bon Marché in Sacramento, and I knew what it cost ($60) because I had seen it advertised in the paper. I see myself making many of the same choices for my daughter.

At the center of this story there is a terrible secret, a kernel of cyanide, and the secret is that the story doesn't matter, doesn't make any difference, doesn't figure. The snow still falls in the Sierra. The Pacific still trembles in its bowl. The great tectonic plates strain against each other while we sleep and wake. Rattlers in the dry grass. Sharks beneath the Golden Gate. In the South they are convinced that they have bloodied their place with history. In the West we do not believe that anything we do can bloody the land, or change it, or touch it.

How could it have come to this?

I am trying to place myself in history.

I have been looking all my life for history and have yet to find it.

The resolutely "colorful," anecdotal quality of San Francisco history. "Characters" abound. It puts one off.

In the South they are convinced that they are capable of having bloodied their land with history. In the West we lack this conviction.

Beautiful country burn again.

The sense of not being up to the landscape.

There in the Ceremonial Courtroom a secular mass was being offered.

. . .

I see now that the life I was raised to admire was infinitely romantic. The clothes chosen for me had a strong element of the Pre-Raphaelite, the medieval. Muted greens and ivories. Dusty roses. (Other people wore powder blue, red, white, navy, forest green, and Black Watch plaid. I thought of them as "conventional," but I envied them secretly. I was doomed to unconventionality.) Our houses were also darker than other people's, and we favored, as a definite preference, copper and brass that had darkened and greened. We also let our silver darken carefully in all the engraved places, "to bring out the pattern." To this day I am disturbed by highly polished silver. It looks "too new."

This predilection for "the old" carried into all areas of our domestic life: dried flowers were seen to have a more lasting charm than fresh, prints should be faded, a wallpaper should be streaked by the sun before it looks right. As decorative touches went, our highest moment was the acquisition of a house (we, the family, moved into it in 1951 at 22nd and T in Sacramento) in which the curtains had not been changed since 1907. Our favorite curtains in this house were gold silk organza on a high window on the stairwell. They hung almost two stories, billowed iridescently with every breath of air, and crumbled at the touch. To our extreme disapproval, Genevieve Didion, our grandmother, replaced these curtains when she moved into the house in the late 1950s. I think of those curtains still, and so does my mother (domestic design).

Oriental leanings. The little ebony chests, the dishes. Maybeck houses. Mists. The individual raised to mystic level, mysticism with no religious basis.

When I read Gertrude Atherton* I recognize the territory of the subtext. The assemblies

* Gertrude Atherton (1857–1948) was born in San Francisco and became a prolific and at times controversial writer of novels, short stories, essays, and articles on subjects that included feminism, politics, and war. Many of her novels are set in California.

unattended, the plantations abandoned—in the novels as in the dreamtime—because of high and noble convictions about slavery. Maybe they had convictions, maybe they did not, but they had also worked out the life of the farm. In the novels as well as the autobiography of Mrs. Atherton we see a provincial caste system at its most malign. The pride in "perfect taste," in "simple frocks."

In the autobiography, page 72, note Mrs. Atherton cutting snakes in two with an axe.

When I read Gertrude Atherton I think not only of myself but of Patricia Hearst, listening to *Carousel* in her room on California Street.

The details of the Atherton life appear in the Atherton fiction, or the details of the fiction appear in the autobiography: it is difficult to say which is the correct construction. The beds of Parma violets at the Atherton house dissolve effortlessly into the beds of Parma violets at Maria Ballinger-Groome Abbott's house in Atherton's *The Sisters-in-Law*. Gertrude's mother had her three-day "blues," as did one of the characters in *Sleeping Fires*. Were there Parma violets at the Atherton house? Did Gertrude's mother have three-day blues?

When I contrast the houses in which I was raised, in California, to admire, with the houses my husband was raised, in Connecticut, to admire, I am astonished that we should have ever built a house together.

Climbing Mount Tamalpais in Marin County, a mystical ideal. I never did it, but I did walk across the Golden Gate Bridge, wearing my first pair of high-heeled shoes, bronze kid De Liso Debs pumps with three-inch heels. Crossing the Gate was, like climbing Tamalpais, an ideal.

Corte Madera. Head cheese. Eating apricots and plums on the rocks at Stinson Beach.

Until I read Gertrude Atherton I had never seen the phrase "South of Market" used exactly the way my grandmother, my mother, and I had always used it. Edmund G. "Pat" Brown was South of Market.

My father and brother call it "Cal" (i.e., the University of California at Berkeley). They were fraternity men, my father a Chi Phi, my brother a Phi Gamma Delta. As a matter of fact I belonged to a house too, Delta Delta Delta, but I lived in that house for only two of the four years I spent at Berkeley.

There used to be a point I liked on the Malibu Canyon road between the San Fernando Valley and the Pacific Ocean, a point from which one could see what was always called "the Fox sky." Twentieth Century-Fox had a ranch back in the hills there, not a working ranch but several thousand acres on which westerns were shot, and "the Fox sky" was simply that: the Fox sky, the giant Fox sky scrim, the Big Country backdrop.

By the time I started going to Hawaii, the Royal Hawaiian was no longer the "best" hotel in Honolulu, nor was Honolulu the "smart" place to vacation in Hawaii, but Honolulu and the Royal Hawaiian had a glamour for California children who grew up as I did. Little girls in Sacramento were brought raffia grass skirts by returning godmothers. They were taught "Aloha 'Oe" at Girl Scout meetings, and to believe that their clumsiness would be resolved via mastery of the hula. For dances, later, they wanted leis, and if not leis, brace-

lets of tiny orchids, "flown in" from Honolulu. I recall "flown in" as a common phrase
of my adolescence in Sacramento, just "flown
in," the point of origin being unspoken, and
implicit. The "luau," locally construed as a
barbecue with leis, was a favored entertain-
ment. The "lanai" replaced the sunporch in
local domestic architecture. The romance
of all things Hawaiian colored my California
childhood, and the Royal Hawaiian seemed to
stand on Waikiki as tangible evidence that this
California childhood had in fact occurred.

I have had on my desk since 1974 a photograph that I cut from a magazine just after
Patricia Campbell Hearst was kidnapped
from her Berkeley apartment. This photograph
appeared quite often around that time, always
credited to Wide World, and it shows Patricia
Hearst and her father and one of her sisters at
a party at the Burlingame Country Club. In this
photograph it is six or seven months before the
kidnapping, and the three Hearsts are smiling
for the camera, Patricia, Anne, and Randolph.

The father is casual but festive—light coat,
dark shirt, no tie; the daughters flank him in

long flowered dresses. They are all wearing leis, father and daughters alike, leis quite clearly "flown in" for the evening. Randolph Hearst wears two leis, one of maile leaves and the other of orchids strung in the tight design the lei-makers call "Maunaloa." The daughters each wear pikake leis, the rarest and most expensive kind of leis, strand after strand of tiny Arabian jasmine buds strung like ivory beads.

Sometimes I have wanted to know what my grandmother's sister, May Daly, screamed the day they took her to the hospital, for it concerned me, she had fixed on me, sixteen, as the source of the terror she sensed, but I have refrained from asking. In the long run it is better not to know. Similarly, I do not know whether my brother and I said certain things to each other at three or four one Christmas morning or whether I dreamed it, and have not asked.

We are hoping to spend part of every summer together, at Lake Tahoe. We are hoping to reinvent our lives, or I am.

The San Francisco Social Register. When did San Francisco become a city with a Social Register? How did this come about? The social ambitiousness of San Francisco, the way it has always admired titles, even bogus titles.

All my life I have been reading these names and I have never known who they were or are. Who, for example, is Lita Vietor?

C. Vann Woodward: "Every self-conscious group of any size fabricates myths about its past: about its origins, its mission, its righteousness, its benevolence, its general superiority." This has not been exactly true in San Francisco.

SOME WOMEN:

Gertrude Atherton
Julia Morgan
Lillie Coit
Jessica Peixotto
Dolly Fritz MacMasters Cope
Lita Vietor
Phoebe Apperson Hearst
Patricia Campbell Hearst
Jessie Benton Frémont

Part of it is simply what looks right to the eye, sounds right to the ear. I am at home in the West. The hills of the coastal ranges look "right" to me, the particular flat expanse of the Central Valley comforts my eye. The place names have the ring of real places to me. I can pronounce the names of the rivers, and recognize the common trees and snakes. I am easy here in a way that I am not easy in other places.

A Note About the Author

Joan Didion was born in California and lives in New York. She is the author of five novels, nine previous books of nonfiction, and a play.

A Note on the Type

This book was set in Bodoni, a typeface named after Giam-battista Bodoni (1740–1813), the celebrated printer and type designer of Parma. Bodoni's innovations in type style included a greater degree of contrast in the thick and thin elements of the letters and a sharper and more angular finish of details.

Typeset by Scribe,

Philadelphia, Pennsylvania

Printed and bound by LSC Communications,

Crawfordsville, Indiana

Designed by Iris Weinstein